333
TIPS
— FOR —
SAILORS

Fridtjof Gunkel, Editor

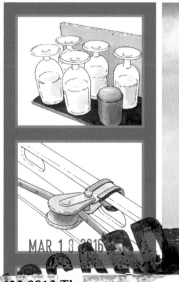

Published by Schiffer Publishing, Ltd.
4880 Lower Valley Road
Atglen, PA 19310
Phone: (610) 593-1777; Fax: (610) 593-2002
E-mail: Info@schifferbooks.com

For our complete selection of fine books on this
and related subjects, please visit our website at
www.schifferbooks.com. You may also write for a
free catalog.

This book may be purchased from the publisher.
Please try your bookstore first.

We are always looking for people to write books on
new and related subjects. If you have an idea for a
book, please contact us at

proposals@schifferbooks.com.

Schiffer Publishing's titles are available at special
discounts for bulk purchases for sales promotions
or premiums. Special editions, including
personalized covers, corporate imprints, and
excerpts can be created in large quantities for
special needs. For more information, contact the
publisher.

CONTENTS

FOREWORD

Sailing is many things: a grandiose hobby, a tough sport, or simply pure relaxation. But sailing can be more: moving along the edge of the two elements, water and air, is a complex motion that keeps two sciences busy, that of hydrodynamics and the related aerodynamics. More complex than sailing as such can be the boat itself with its many components. After all, it is a vehicle that has to unite many different things: it is at the same time a vehicle and a habitat, a small autonomous and technical microcosm.

There are complex systems for managing the sails, anchoring, and steering, as well as for electricity, water, and wastewater. Furthermore, a seagoing yacht requires safety equipment, a working pantry, navigation, storage space, bunks, and a wetroom. And, despite this complexity, or perhaps because of it, even a fully-equipped boat delivered by a shipyard is far from satisfying all of the owner's expectations.

It is very clear: every boat has ample room for improvement—and that is a good thing! Simply by optimizing, building, coming up with things, and turning them into reality, customizing the boat to your personal requirements and preferences, as well as to your personal sailing style, is a lot of fun. Most improvements on board will be the result of your own preferences. Another major source for improvements on board, or for maneuvers, comes from observations at the port, the mooring, and at sea.

Take advantage of the ideas that we have collected for you in this book. They consist of the best tips from sailors published by *Yacht,* for fellow sailors, which have helped in many instances.

MOORING & ANCHORING

PARK INSTEAD OF CIRCLING

When sailing in places like the Netherlands, sailors are used to long waiting times at bridges and locks. The few places to park are quickly taken, and the rest of the boats have to maneuver in the very tight space that remains. Most skippers try to park with their bow to the wind, which is almost impossible without accelerating at least a little. So, the most daring donut maneuvers are being performed, increasing the chances of stress and collisions occurring.

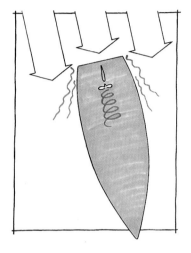

With our Moody 346, we prefer a method where the wind is used as the helmsman: we slowly steer the stern into the wind and keep it in place with short engine bursts. As the point of propulsion now lies windward, the boat behaves like a wind vane while stopped; hardly any corrections are necessary. This works similarly when there is a current.

ROLF KIEPE, 64546 MOERFELDEN

USING THE SPRING TO GET INTO THE BOX MORE EASILY

Many skippers forget that a spring (line) can be very helpful for mooring a boat safely. Not only does it make the helmsman's life easier while putting out to sea during landward winds (see YACHT 25/02) or when putting out or mooring with sidewinds ("Roman-Catholic" style) without stress (see YACHT 23/04), but it is also helpful when entering an unfamiliar box. In case there are no lateral guiding lines, or there is no neighboring boat leewards to "lean on" temporarily with the fender, or if the crew is not well-synchronized or you may be by yourself, you can quickly find yourself askew of the poles rather than with the bow at the jetty during strong sidewinds. This is why we have the following strategy: first, fix a line at the bow and stern; the other mooring lines can be tightened later. Using a spring between the windward stern pole and clamp, or winch, the position of the boat can be controlled nicely with some practice. The main issue is to balance the forces between the engine's forward push and the slipping spring.

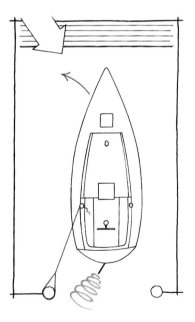

GUNTER HOLTAPPELS, 53197 BONN

MOORING QUICKLY WITHOUT HASSLES

I often sail single-handedly with my Willing 31 and I came up with a simple trick to moor alongside jetties, quays, or other vessels, and with very good results. Of course, I put out the fenders before mooring; they are important for stabilizing the boat when using my method. I place a short end of some 2.5 feet on my cleat and put it over the rail. Then I steer the boat alongside, stop, and use one quick movement to hook the end as shortly as possible to the bollard or cleat, which I have scouted previously. The remaining

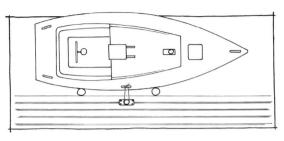

stern and bow lines are placed without a hurry. Of course, the "helper" needs to be removed later.

FRITZ KELLER, 22850 NORDERSTEDT

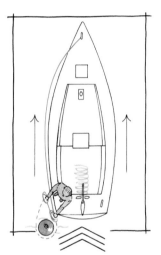

ONE-HANDED TO THE BUOY

Single-handed sailors have to come up with quite a few tricks to make up for the absence of helping hands. In order to tie up to a buoy, I got used to always steering backwards with the stern. This makes it a lot easier to steer the boat in case of strong winds or currents, as the bow steers like a wind vane. I can also reach the buoy much more easily from the stern. First, I place the bow mooring line outboard astern. Idling the engine, I keep the boat with the stern next to the buoy, in place, and tie the lines. It pivots by itself into place.

HANS PRESS, BY EMAIL

ONE-HANDED TO THE JETTY

If you sail by yourself regularly, you need to come up with something to moor the boat. In such a case, I prefer to go alongside a pier or jetty, even with offshore wind. It does not make sense to moor with the bow when you're by yourself because the boat starts moving away immediately after stopping. To move with the stern against the wind, however, has many advantages. The hull straightens itself just like a pendulum. On top of that, not only can you approach the jetty by regulating the engine—down to an inch—you can also keep it almost motionless on its place to throw the line over the cleat, or bollard. Using the winch or center cleat, I pull the bow towards the jetty going forward.

GUNTER HOLTAPPELS, 53279 BONN

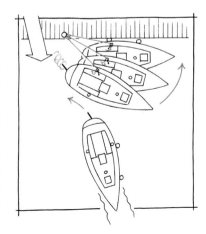

STRAIGHT INTO THE BOX

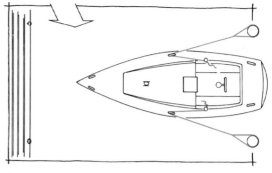

In the case of strong sidewinds, it is difficult to moor inside the box. The yacht may be pushed leeward and damage neighboring boats. It is easier to control the boat when the stern lines are not tied at the stern, but placed amidships over cleats or shackles, onto the winches. As soon as the mooring posts are amidships while entering, both stern lines are fixed and tightened. Then, use the engine to push against the posts, and the boat is maneuvered to the jetty by veering the stern lines.

UDO TENNIGKEIT, 28876

BOX WITH A BRAKE

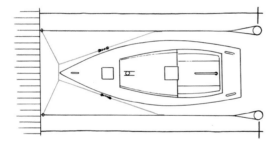

Getting into the box is easier with the following line system. We have added two additional lines to the conventional lines between the mooring posts and the jetty, at about the center of the box. They feature one shock absorber each. Connect these two lines with a cross line in front of the bow. The resulting funnel pulls the bow into the box automatically, while the cross lines guide the boat via the shock absorbers. The distance between the cross line and the jetty must be such so you can get off the boat without the bow bouncing towards the jetty. This system works well for our boat, which has a fairly steep bow.

KARL-HEINZ TEINER, 22927 GROSSHANSDORF

HOSE AS A BOLLARD CATCHER

While at port we often maneuver from bollard to bollard. To do this, we have modified our boathook by unscrewing its head and placing over it a strip of aluminum with a hole in it and two slits at the ends. Slightly bend the flanks of the metal sheet, place a piece of fabric hose through the slits, and close them with rivets. Just screw on the head with the loop in place.

DIETER BEHERENS, 30655 HANNOVER

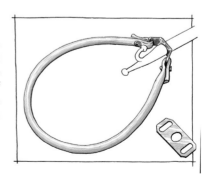

MOORING LINE IN A TUBE

If you are by yourself and need to moor inside a box with stern poles, you need to be fast: stop the boat, place stern lines over the poles, take up speed, put out fenders, stop once the boat is inside the box, and then fasten the bow lines. In order not to take out all the momentum of the boat while doing this maneuver, I have put a simple plastic tube over the stern lines. With the help of these readily available tubes, I can now place the lines, while going past them, without jumping from one side to the other. As

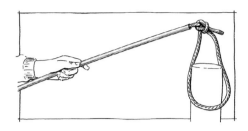

soon as the ship is moored, you can remove the tubes and store them away.

ANSGAR DUEKER, 67487 MAIKAMMER

LARGE LOOP

I read about Ansgar Dueker's tip ("Mooring Line in a Tube") in your 10/2004 edition and immediately copied it. It became obvious right away that there is quite some skill required to catch the pole—the loop is simply too flat. I sawed the tube lengthwise and then heated the plastic with a lighter, which spread the ends. Then I pressed at several places of these resulting half-tubes, and the lighter was quite helpful here as well. This way, the mooring line is literally pinched and opens the loop. Now it is really child's play to place the loop over the poles.

UWE ANDRESEN, 24944 FLENSBURG

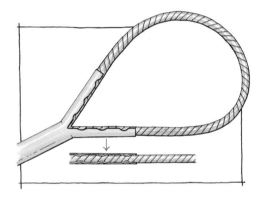

LONG ARMS FOR THE MOORING LINES

If the pole is too far away to place the line by hand, a boathook is quite handy. However, you have to be experienced to succeed with your first try. If you place a metal tongue at the hook, which works like a cleat, or you use cable ties to affix a clothespin, you are certain to be successful.

KLAUS WOLTERS, 41747 VIERSEN, REINER BIELENBERG, 22529 HAMBURG

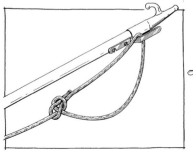
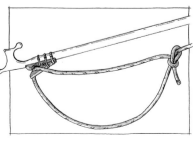

MOORING MADE EASY WHILE LEAVING SPACE

If the box is very wide, we only use one pole, so boats arriving later have space while they undertake mooring and leaving. One line at the stern is sufficient. Using a stern line to the jetty, the boat is kept away from the leeward neighbor.

STEFFI VON WOLFF, BY EMAIL

MOORING AT A VACANT SPACE WITH SOFT DRIFT

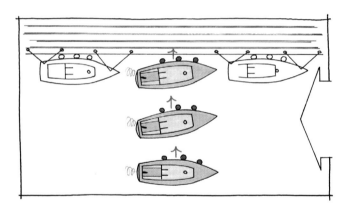

With offshore wind this is quite easy—mooring perpendicularly to the jetty with a prepared bow line, tying it, and then fixing a long stern line to pull the boat to the jetty. Should the space prove to be too small you may talk to your neighbor and ask him to pull the lines a little tighter, or just leave by drifting away from the jetty. If the wind blows landward towards the jetty, we stop at the height of the vacant space with the fenders placed and drift with the wind towards the jetty. While approaching the jetty it becomes obvious whether the vacant space is sufficient or whether you should pull out backwards.

Particularly during the busy vacation periods you often see that not all of the empty spaces are utilized in a full port. If there is only the slightest doubt, not-so-experienced skippers prefer to moor in a pack rather than risking an unsuccessful mooring maneuver. Such vacant spaces often occur at jetties where the crews of the yachts moored alongside have been too generous with the bow and stern lines. This could be easily corrected by tightening the lines a little, but it is often overlooked.

So, the thing left for the newcomer is to use his good judgment and pick the vacant space.

If the wind or the current is parallel to the jetty, we keep the boat hovering in place and slightly steer the bow towards the jetty while the wind or the current pushes the boat towards the intended space—no stress, no hurry.

HANS-HENNING KOEHLER, 21745 HEMMOOR

GOOD SOLUTION: MOORING FOR EMERGENCIES

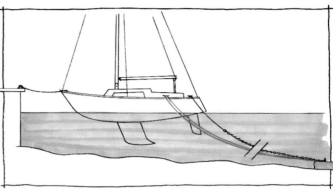

Anchoring with the help of mooring lines is very common in the Mediterranean. But what are the conditions of the equipment in the water? Often the chains are corroded and the lines may be in bad shape. Nobody knows whether they will withstand the next storm. The bow lines are clearly visible, but they don't hold the boat away from the jetty. Because we have to leave our yacht unattended for long periods of time, I was looking for other methods to secure our boat. The concrete block at a depth of some ten feet was heavy and stable enough. I affixed a heavy shackle with an additional strong halyard. I have reeved it so it can be checked from the boat for defects, abrasions or growth. The main load is still on the old chain; the line is to provide safety.

FRITZ KELLER, 22850 NORDERSTEDT

COMFORTABLY TO THE MOORING

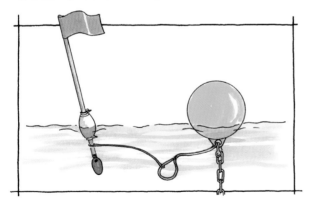

Our yacht is usually at a mooring. Because I often sail single-handed, the process has to be as simple as possible. In order to catch the heavy loop at the buoy more easily, we built ourselves an auxiliary buoy. Place a floater from a fishing net onto a 5-foot-long PCV pipe; use two cable ties to affix the floater to the tube, one above and one below. Put a lead weight, available at fishing equipment retailers, at the lower end of the PVC pipe. Affix a bright flag to the upper end of the pipe. Tie the completed auxiliary buoy to the eye of the mooring with a thin line. When you approach the mooring, you won't need to fish around with the boathook, as you can grab the upper end of the auxiliary buoy comfortably from the deck without inconveniencing yourself. The cost of the necessary material is only a few dollars.

FRANK SAUER, 598699 SINGAPORE

AUXILIARY LOOP FOR MOORING

When mooring at a bollard, the main feat is to place the line safely across the pole. More so if you prefer to place one line over a bollard and then sway along the long line to tie down the boat. In order to secure the line at the boathook, we use an auxiliary loop. We use a long boathook and put on a long line. At about the center of the line we knot a sliding loop. Now the mooring halyard can be securely placed over the bollard with the boathook. Pull the hook out of the loop and pull the loose end of the line tight. While doing this, the loop will slide out by itself and the line can be veered without getting stuck when leaving.

GABRIELE MUEHLHOFF, 42349 WUPPERTAL

LINE ON A LONG HOOK

We sail primarily in the Aegean Sea. There, mooring is done "Roman-Catholic" style, with the bow anchor and the stern to the jetty. Small crews and single-handed sailors both encounter the problem of having no one to take care of the stern lines. We have solved this by making a stainless-steel hook out of a half-inch, strong, round material. The hook is fitted with an 8-foot line and placed on a stern cleat. In most cases there are steel bows set into the concrete of the jetty where we can place our hook. Right after stopping the boat, you can moor without

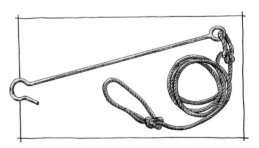

leaving the boat. Then you just set up the gangway and take your time to tie the regular stern lines.

KLEMENS MEIER, 8440 PAROS/GREECE

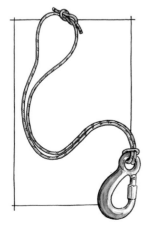

HOOK LINE FOR CLEAN HANDS

In many instances, mooring lines are caught with the boathook, pulled out of the water, and led to the bow hand-over-hand. But they are often dirty and full of mussels. We use a snap hook tied to a line loop. You pick up the line, snap in the carabiner and use it to pull the line towards the bow. There, you place the loop over the cleat and pull in the mooring line. If it slips from your hand, the hook catches it, making it easy to pull it in.

TORSTEN BERGER, 02906 NIESKY

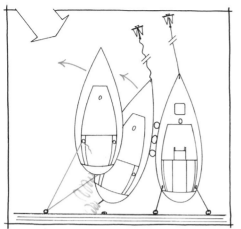

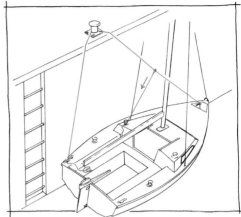

HELP WITH STRONG WIND

If you have to moor "Roman-Catholic" style, as is common in the Mediterranean, you depend on your anchor. It is quite common that increasing sidewinds or increasing pressure from windward neighboring boats can cause the anchor to break out and push the boat against the jetty or the leeward neighbor. Now you have to act quickly.

The only effective measure here is to fix a windward line—with a few turns around the sheet winch—that can be veered under your control. This causes the endangered stern to get away from the jetty and may stabilize the yacht in its position by regulating the engine so that the boat stays in place against the wind. Now you can take your time to decide whether you want to sail after pulling in the anchor. In this case it makes sense to place the line around a bollard on the jetty (put it on slip) and have the other line tight on deck. The other option— provided the line is long enough—is to drive leeward to place the anchor again and increase its holding power with a suitable sliding weight.

GUNTER HOLTAPPELS, 53179 BONN

HELP AT THE LOCK

During our last vacation we went through several locks with our smallish Waarschip 570. Because we are of advanced age, we wanted to minimize the dangerous maneuvering on the narrow foredeck. So, we have a long line on one of the cleats inside of the small, open anchor box at the bow that we place around the lock bollard, and veer it, using the stern cleat, which can be handled comfortably from the cockpit. On the front section of this guiding line we also run a kind of auxiliary line with a threaded thimble, which is practical for more than just controlling this section of the line: as soon as we are done in the lock, this line is also helpful for taking in the guiding line without having to step onto the foredeck.

WILFRIED KORFF, 40489 DUESSELDORF

KEEPING IT QUIET

The night could be so peaceful while at anchor, were it not for the line of the anchor making noise at the bow, slipping back and forth. The result is loud creaking sounds below deck. If there is too much slack, the result can sound like a hammer. We have taken care of the matter with a wood block that we have prepared for this purpose. The block sits with its two grooves on the anchor bracket and is secured with a piece of string. Instead of slipping over the roll, the line now lies firmly inside a groove of the wood block. To avoid chafing, a piece of rubber hose is placed around the line.

WOLFGANG WELKE, 44137 DORTMUND

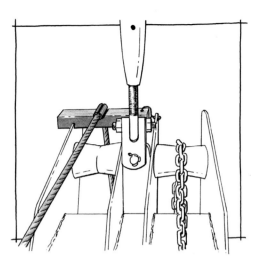

SIMPLE SLIDING WEIGHT

A sliding weight increases the anchor's holding force and diminishes the swerve. Our cost-effective version consists of a robust plastic bottle we have filled with lead weights (available at tire shops). The remaining float is eliminated by filling it with water. If you use polyester instead of water, the small lead weights are fixed as well. Close the bottle using some sealant. This handy sliding weight weighs about 12 lbs. and is clipped to the line with a carabiner.

INGEBORG CLASEN, 22605 HAMBURG

PROTECTION AGAINST JELLYFISH

You might have noticed that jellyfish are an increasingly frequent nuisance when sailing. Not only do they ruin the joys of bathing, they are also a problem when anchoring. Our anchor has some fifteen feet of chain and a halyard, and has to be recovered hand-over-hand, no winch. If there are threads of jellyfish, even brushing them will not help much. The result is

quite painful skin rashes that hurt for days. We tried household rubber gloves, but they were not durable. We found that work gloves with rubber-coated and nubbed-interior sides are best. If you pay a little more, you can keep your hands dry by getting a waterproof model.

UWE ANDRESEN, 40255 DUESSELDORF

PREDETERMINED BREAKING POINT

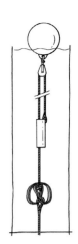

The line of an anchor buoy can sometimes become stuck to the drifting boat. If the wind increases, there is a risk of the anchor breaking out. We have devised a predetermined breaking point using an old car tire tube. As shown in the drawing, it is incorporated into the lower section of the line. Its upper end is threaded through two holes of the ring and knotted in such a way that they let the knot slip through when the pull increases.

KLAUS EBERT, 70197 STUTTGART

BOAT LADDER AS ANCHOR HELPER

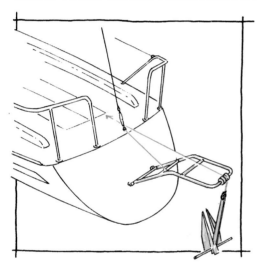

Our boat does not have an anchor locker, so we run the anchor from the stern. The only problem: the anchor can easily scratch and damage the coat during any maneuver; the chain in particular is prone to leave scars. This can be avoided by making an anchor roll from plastic. We have placed these rolls onto the lowest rung of the ladder. When anchoring, we simply lower the ladder with a line until it is about horizontal to the water and then we let the chain and halyard slide over the roll. This way, the anchor doesn't damage the boat's surface.

JAN KNECHT, BY EMAIL

MOORING WITH THE BUOY LASSO

We have a trick for making it easier to get to the mooring buoy. Prepare a loop with a fairly short line. While the helmsman steers the bow towards the buoy and past it, the bowman throws the lasso over the buoy and carefully hauls tight. If you leave, spread the loop with two people using the boathook so it can be pulled over the buoy. The helmsman returns to the rudder and you're done.

OTTO KALKBRENNER, 8010 GRAZ/AUSTRIA

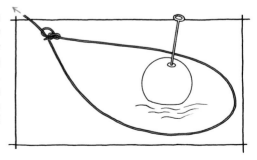

ANCHOR LINE AT THE SNOUT

Yachts with a fixed gennaker cannot really take advantage of a guiding roll for the anchor line at the bow, because the line should not run over the bow, but over the bowsprit. If the anchor line runs over the bow into the water, it will shear at the bobstay while the boat is swerving. We have found the following solution: a large aluminum carabiner is fixed onto a thin line, which runs to the bowsprit. Once the anchor is set and firm, we clip the carabiner to the anchor line and pull it to the bow. This also works when mooring at buoys.

CHRISTIAN FEIGE, 94469 DEGGENDORF

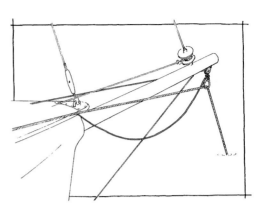

CLEAN CHAIN

If you have to anchor at muddy places, you already know the problem: the anchor sinks into the mud and holds well, but the next morning the chain is usually completely soiled and difficult to clean with a brush. So, we took two scrubbers and screwed them together onto a broom stick, with the bristles face to face. When we pull up the anchor, we simply run the chain through the brushes. The result is pretty effective.

EDGAR WOHLHEBEN, BY EMAIL

SIMPLE TRICK TO PREVENT CHAFING

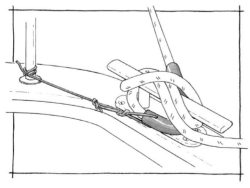

There are numerous methods sailors use to protect their lines from sharp concrete or rock edges. We keep a couple of robust pieces of rubber hose of some two feet that have been cut open lengthwise, like a spiral. I usually cut one turn every four or five inches—this works pretty well. When they are needed, we wrap them around the line in a spiral and secure both ends with safety cables so they don't move out of position. If conditions are extreme, you can position another larger piece of hose onto the line, one which has been cut up in the opposite direction.

PETER SPARGEL, 22047 HAMBURG

BUOY WITH REMOTE RELEASE

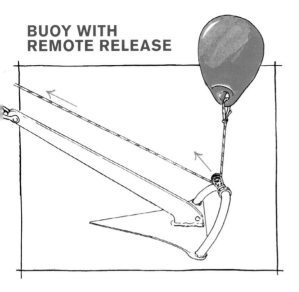

There are several methods for indicating the location of the anchor. Most of them have the disadvantage that when you lift the anchor, you have to haul in additional lines. They can easily get entangled with the anchor chain and get caught by the propeller. We clipped a block to our anchor. The plastic clip is actually used for the installation of tubing. When putting out the anchor, we just put the buoy out with it. Once the anchor has taken hold, the length of the line can be adjusted so the buoy is floating over it. Before we take in the anchor, we pull the buoy under the water up to the block and release the clip with a strong pull. The buoy, the block, and the line can now be retrieved one by one.

ANSGAR DUEKER, 67487 MAIKAMMER

HELP WITH ANCHOR RECOVERY

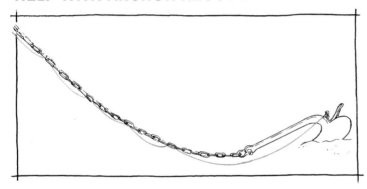

We have threaded a line through every fifth chain link of our anchor, up until about three feet from the anchor itself. We can now recover the anchor without diving, even if it is stuck. We recover the anchor line, and once the anchor chain appears, so does our auxiliary halyard. With a little pulling and letting go, the shaft of the anchor becomes loose and usually sets the anchor free.

DIETER BEHRENS, 30665 HANNOVER

RUNNING LOOP

If you use lines around the stern pole, either doubling them or using a bowline, you often have to pick them out of the dirty port water the next day, because they slide down when there is no pull on them. This can easily be avoided. With a running loop (see drawing) at the center of the doubled line you can place the line at any height of the pole by pulling at line A. Just make sure that the section A line is the one that is tightened when tying to the cleat. If you use a bowline at the small loop, the pole loop is prevented from becoming too tight, even with a lot of tension. When you leave, simply pull on

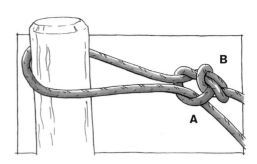

part B of the line and, once loose, snap the line so that it slips off from the pole.

WERNER HOTEL, 74564 CRAILSHEIM

REMOTE CONTROL WITH BRAKE

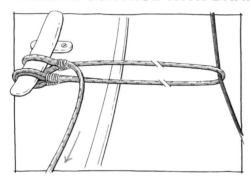

While the connection sling is running on the guiding line, as with the variant shown here in the accompanying illustration, this method can be used at unfamiliar moorings. The last eyelet on the cleat contains a tightly-fitting rubber loop so it does not slip off at the wrong moment.

DIETER JUNGE, 24837 SCHLESWIG

REMOTE CONTROL FOR THE AUXILIARY LINE

If you are a single-handed sailor, you know about this problem: when putting out to sea from a box, the bow remains uncontrolled for quite some time, as there is a moment between loosening the halyards and when the boat picks up speed. With leader lines set to slip, the maneuver can be controlled much better, but the long end will end up in the water after loosening and might get caught by the propeller. For this reason, I utilize a retrieval line, which can be used in many situations. With one loop around the leader line, it can be doused from the cockpit. Additionally, the lateral guiding (pilot) line can be pulled from the clamp from astern.

HARTWIG CARSTENSEN, 21035 HAMBURG

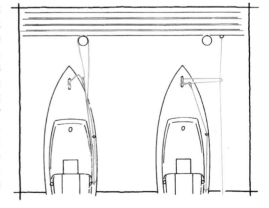

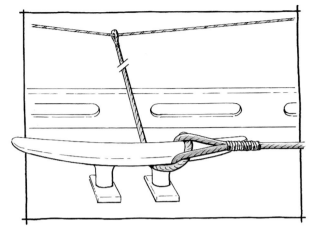

REMOTE RELEASE

Single-handed maneuvers, such as dropping out from the box during strong sidewinds, requires some clever thinking. In order to release the eyelet of the connecting sling between the lateral guiding line and the foreship cleat from astern, I place the eyelet of a thin line in front of the lateral line over the cleat. All it takes is one pull to release it.

SEEN IN SONDERBORG

BOWLINE WITHOUT A ROPE END

There are several methods available for putting a loop that doesn't tighten, and can easily be loosened, right into a section of a line with no rope end available (for example, while towing several boats). Take a section of line and double it, making a figure-eight knot—which can actually tighten quite easily. If you take some more slack from the doubled line, it is easy to make a conventional bowline. You can also try my bowline method: I think this is something new. I place an eyelet through the front section of the doubled line, then thread the rear section in from below with a small loop. By doing this, I'm actually pulling the large eyelet from the rear all the way through and flipping the small loop I threaded first towards the incoming and outgoing sections. If you proceed exactly as shown in the drawing, and tighten the knot, you get a slightly modified bowline. It does not tighten even under heavy stress, from whichever direction, and can be opened as easily as the classic version by flipping the small loop towards the front.

TUFAN TUERKILERI, 50823 COLOGNE

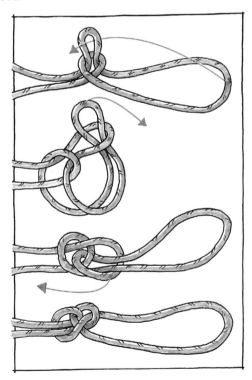

COMBINED SHOCK ABSORBER AND CHAFING PROTECTION

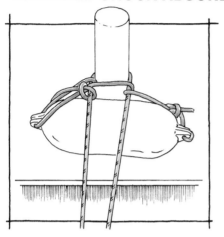

When we went on our journey to Sweden, we found out that many of the ports and skerries only had steel rings or low bollards set into the concrete floor or the rock, not far from the quay wall. The rough edges can quickly chafe and damage the mooring lines, more so if there is a swell, making for an unsteady stay. For this reason, I have come up with the following: I place a small fender under the mooring line and affix it to the bollard or the ring. Used in this way, it provides both protection against chafing of the lines as well as shock absorption.

ARTUR WEINEKOETTER, 59302 OELDE

WET BARRIER

After we repeatedly witnessed that bugs were crawling over our mooring line onto the boat, we needed a quick solution. Because the usual rat traps do not necessarily keep ants and other crawling bugs away, we came up with a wet solution: the sliding weight on the bow mooring lines keeps the lines under water. Another advantage of this method is the shock-absorbing feature.

SIEGFRIED TROPPER, 73054 EISLINGEN

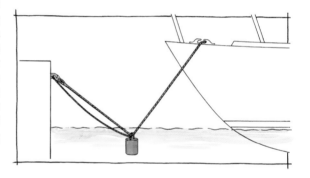

SLIP-PROOF BOWLINE

If a bowline is disproportionately weighted, the loop may slip, particularly if the lines are modern, new, and smooth. If you slip the end of the line as shown, you get a slip-proof loop.

ILHAMNI BARLAK, 51373 LEVERKUSEN

TAKING OFF THE EDGE OF THE BOLLARD

As is the case with so many sailing yachts, our Sun Odyssey 32.2 has exposed bow navigation lights, which are prone to breaking when they touch bollards, poles, or lock walls. It almost always requires getting a replacement. This is a bothersome and expensive design flaw. In our case it was not possible to modify the setup, so we had to come up with another solution to protect the expensive and essential lights. We bent two stainless-steel sections so that they protect the lights when maneuvering at port, by screwing them to the tubing of the pulpit. To further increase their stability, we welded a brace lengthwise into the arch.

HERMANN BOEHM, 53797 LOHMAR

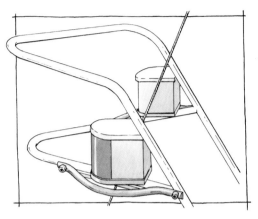

QUICKMOUNT FOR SHOCK ABSORBER

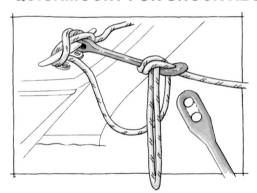

We use our mooring lines without a shock absorber. In order to quickly put them on, we cut off the section between the two holes of a shock absorber so we can run the mooring line with a loop through them and tie it to the sheet bend. The other end is fixed with a mooring line on a cleat.

HEINZ DIETER JUNGE, 24837 SCHLESWIG

SECURE BOWLINE

An improved classic. Tie the knot as usual, keeping the loose end long enough so as to wrap it once around the loop and then put it back through the eye once more.

MARKUS BAGGENSTOS,
4900 LANGENTHAL/SWITZERLAND

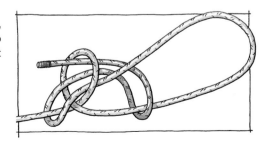

RAM PROTECTION

It is not always possible to avoid serious contact between the quay wall and the anchor or the bow fitting. If you are using a plough anchor, you can use a medium-size ball fender as a shock absorber.

CHRISTOPH BAUER, 93413 CHAM

OUTBOARD MOTOR WITH RUDDER ACTION

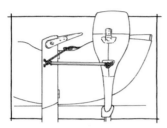

You can latch the motor to the rudder with one pull when maneuvering in a harbor.

If you have an outboard engine at the stern, you have good steering at port. If there is not sufficient space, you can simply turn the motor

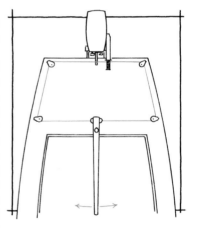

with the rudder, and the yacht will spin in place. In order to have this additional maneuverability always available, we have latched the engine to the rudder. Affix a small metal bracket to the back of the outboard with a screw while adding a firm eye bracket to the rudder, also using screws. Next, cut a section of stainless steel or plastic tubing so that it fits between the engine and the rudder. The connection between the two is via a threaded line, which is affixed to a cam cleat on board. The trick here is the following: as long as the line has tension, the motor stays connected to the rudder; if the line is loosened, the tube swings downwards, the engine can be tilted, and the rudder works just as before.

DIETER BEHRENS, 30655 HANNOVER

CAM CLEATS AS AUXILIARY CLEATS

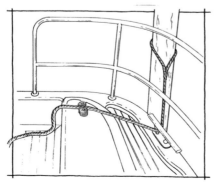

The wide sterns of modern yachts are a disadvantage when mooring in a box. To facilitate things we run the stern lines through the stern cleats, close to the helmsman, and fix them with cam cleats on the coaming. This allows for the stern lines to be quickly tied or loosened. Once the boat lies in the box the way it should, tie down the lines on the cleats.

JOACHIM HEITMANN, 23779 NEUKIRCHEN

UNIVERSAL CHAIN CLAW

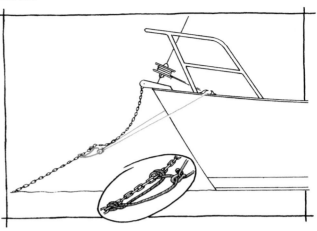

When you relieve the anchor, you spare the passengers in the bow cabin the rattling of the chain. By using a chain sling, you can accomplish this and diminish jerking during strong winds, which stabilizes the boat as well. However, many chartered boats do not include the line as part of their equipment. Because there are so many different sizes of chains, it is difficult to choose a suitable hook to take with you. Instead, we use an old section of line and make a loop of about a foot in diameter with a splice. Wrap the loop three or four times around the chain. Next, we connect them with a bridle. Place the ends of the line on their respective bow cleats so that the shackle hangs right in front of the bow. Veer the anchor chain until it has some slack above the knot and the pull is on the lines. This not only provides for better sleep, the boat also sways less.

HANS-GERHARD KOCH, 44309 DORTMUND

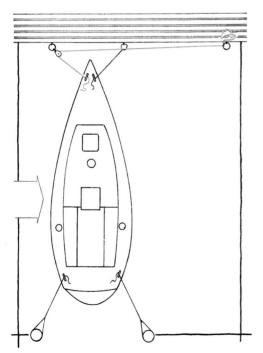

MOORING ON A LONG LINE

Shock absorbers have their limits and they are not always handy when you need them. This is why we use an extra-long line when the port is choppy, preferably from laid rope. Place it at the windward pole and redirect it with a block, parallel to the jetty, to the next box (one after the other). The long line decreases the jerking of the boat significantly and provides pleasant calmness on board.

ROBERT SELTRECHT, BY EMAIL

COMFORT & COCKPIT

EXTRA TABLE FOR SMALL COCKPITS

When a crew consists of more than four people, it can get rather cramped in the cockpit when having breakfast. Although the thwarts offer enough seating space for everyone, the standard cockpit tables offer much too little space for food and beverages.

So, for the area behind the wheel in my Hallberg-Rassy 39, I built an additional item, which is stored upright in the locker when not in use, taking up little space. I added two wooden blocks to the side of the table—they prevent the table from slipping down the spokes of the wheel. I drilled a hole through these blocks and the frame of the table and inserted a long threaded bolt. A wooden brace supports the table at the wheel, and two butterfly nuts affix it to the bolt.

This way you have enough space to offer comfort for two additional people on board

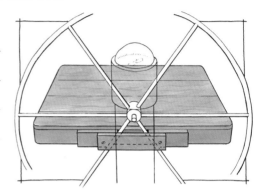

whenever you need it. To avoid falling items, don't forget to block the wheel before serving any food.

FRIEDHELM GOECKE, 58332 SCHWELM

TABLE FOR GUESTS INSTEAD OF WHEEL

Our cockpit table only offers enough space for four people. In order to host more people we have mounted an additional table behind the steering column. The wheel needs to be removed first. The front edge of the table features a block of wood with a hole of the same size as the diameter of the wheel axle. At the back, the plate rests on top of the cockpit thwart. The extra space offers room for two people or for placing food and beverages.

LUDGER ARENS, 59320 ENNIGERLOH

CUSTOMIZED TABLE

Stock boats usually have tables that are either too large or too small. If you want to use the available space in the most comprehensive way, you should consider a custom solution. We did so with an item for our Delanta 78 by gluing together alternating teak sections and narrow ash wood strips. We have added two lateral plates to the basic table, which can be tilted, of course. The table is stored with a homemade support with hinges, which is fixed to the head of the rudder shaft after lifting up the helm. An X-shaped folding support provides the necessary stability, which is increased further with a line to the eye of the main sheet. Whenever we don't need the table at port, we just flip it up and lean it at the crowfoot of the backstay, which requires veering the pulley quickly and hauling it tight again.

ARM IN HORN, 71272 RENNINGEN

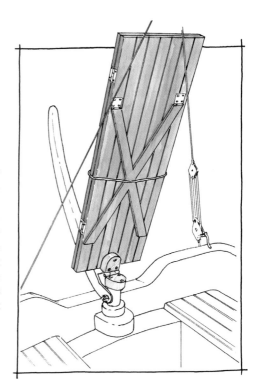

MORE SPACE AT THE SMALL TABLE

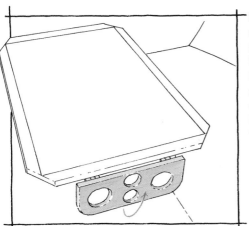

Space on our little cruiser is not abundant; less so once the salon table is set up. Because we need more room while eating but did not want to compromise the available space any further, I added a folding cup holder. The openings match the glasses and cups on board and thus avoid slippage. The holder is fixed via a sliding latch and held in place with two hinges.

WILDFRIED KORFF, BY EMAIL

MULTIFUNCTIONAL BOARD FOR COCKPIT

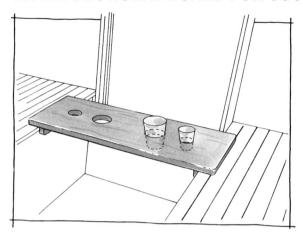

Where do you put full glasses and cups so they don't fall over? We built a tray for our Waarship 570 that not only holds the containers in place, but can also be transported. With the addition of two ledges, it can be stored between the cockpit thwarts without slipping, in case of heeling. If your board is strong enough or reinforced with ledges, the board may be used as a comfortable seat at the ladderway or as a fender board.

WILFRIED KORFF, 40489 DUESSELDORF

TABLE AS A HATCH

Usually a two-part hatch provides enough protection against wind and rain. If the trip leads to rougher open seas, this method is not quite optimal, or so thought the Swede Marcus Krell aboard his Albin Vega "Dory." To make sure that breakers from astern would not flood the salon, he replaced the original hatch with a stable plywood plate, which overlaps at the outside. While looking for a storage space for the solid hatch, he had the idea that the large plate would make for a good salon table. So, he simply fitted the inside of the new hatch with a readily available table support. He added the corresponding counterparts in the salon and the cockpit. This way, the heavy weather hatch is easy to use and store, and also can be set up in the cockpit while at port or anchoring.

SEEN ON THE SWEDISH YACHT "DORY".

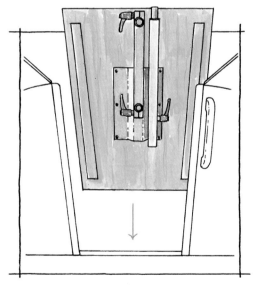

GANGWAY WITH TWO USES

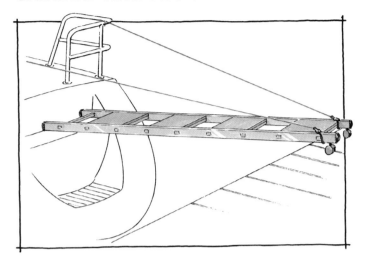

In order to reach land more comfortably from the stern of our boat, we decided to build our own gangway, as those offered by retailers seemed to be too heavy, too expensive, and too unwieldy. We thought a simple wooden board was rather unsophisticated and not solid enough.

So, we went to a building supplies store and bought a simple aluminum ladder of some eight feet in length for about 70 dollars, having nine rungs and two turning plastic wheels, which we screwed to the bottom of the stringers at one end. Then we had four plywood boards of identical size cut out (half an inch thick, about one foot by one foot) and, after treating them with varnish, we clipped them between the stringers, leaving every other stringer empty. They stay in place, but if you want to be extra careful, you can affix them with two screws.

Use two thin guiding lines, shackles, and carabiners between the end of the ladder and the stern pulpit to fix the gangway laterally. This way we get a stable and easy-to-manage bridge to the quay. While sailing we store the gangway along the railing and tie it down. The other use it offers: if we take the boat out of the water we always have a ladder handy, with which we don't have to remove the boards, as you can easily step on the ladder using every second rung.

ACHIM WECKLER, 63263 NEU-ISENBURG

SECURE FOOTING

Many cockpits feature a threaded shaft for the table. However, the long table leg creates a strong lever arm, so there are always leaks. Our construction is a lot more stable: an aluminum profile is fitted with a wide base and affixed to the traveler track with a u-shaped, threaded clamp and wing bolts. Advantage: a quick setup and takedown as well as no risk of leakages.

HERMANN DUENHOELTER, 22529 HAMBURG

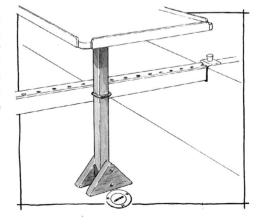

GETTING ON BOARD THE EASY WAY

We started sailing fairly late and got our licenses when we retired. We bought a dinghy cruiser and found a berth at Lake Ploener. However, compared to medical doctors, health insurance agencies, and insurance companies, we found out that boat manufacturers do not really think about their customers getting older. Getting onboard via the bow pulpit forestay, in particular, proved to be rather difficult, so we decided to develop a bow platform that would allow us to get on board while carrying a bag and not get all bent out of shape. The bow platform consists of a thick plywood section, which was cut, glued, and screwed together following the shape of the bow and scuff rail. Two stainless-steel brackets hold onto the crossbar, while the base plate reaching onto the deck is secured with two large sash locks.

Unfortunately, the anchor, purchased as an accessory, proved to be unsuitable, so we bought a heavier anchor with a chain forerun and a thicker cable. Handling it on the narrow foredeck proved to be more difficult than with the original anchor. In order to avoid anchoring maneuvers becoming stressful, particularly lifting the anchor, I added two rollers to the bow step. I used two

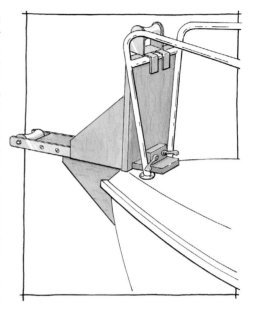

old bicycle hubs from my raw material collection. Of course you may simply buy regular bow rollers at a boating supplies store.

GERHARD BAHR, 22559 HAMBURG

BOW LADDER AND GENNAKER TIP

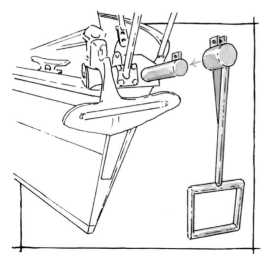

In order to get the lightweight sail away from the mainsail, we have soldered a short, stainless-steel tube as a gennaker boom at the bow fitting. A piece of flat material at the top serves as the anchor point for the line. The trick here is the bow step, which is slipped on. While at port, slide it over the tube and secure it with a bolt. If you are worried about thieves, use a padlock instead of a bolt. We determined the height of the step beforehand so we only need one of them.

HANS-JOACHIM KUTZ, 13403 BERLIN

REMOVABLE STEP

Deep cockpits provide a sense of security as the sailor is not as exposed to the elements. The disadvantage is, when you quickly want to get into the cabin over the gangboard, you need to make more of a leap than a step. For this reason I wanted to add a step. The problem: if you sit at the table in the cockpit, the step should not be in the way of your feet, so it had to be removable. So, I cut two wooden boards, which are affixed to the lateral walls of the cockpit and form the step. The gap between the cockpit wall and the ledges allows for the two boards to be stored away when not in use.

HARMUT STEINKUEHL, 47443 MOERS

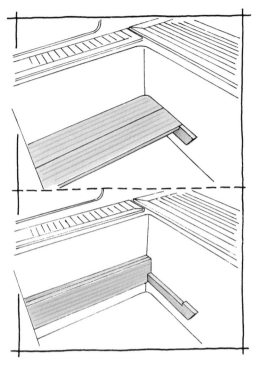

NEW STERN ACCESS

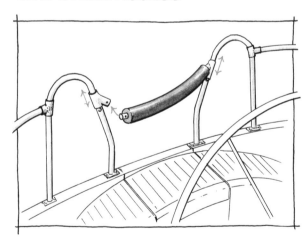

Our Sun Odyssey 32.2 had a six-and-a-half-foot-long wire between the stern railing handles, which was too unsafe and uncomfortable for the helmsman to lean on. We mounted two additional bails left and right of the access to the bathing platform. We replaced the wire with firm tubes as the cross section. They were mounted using T-shaped socket-pipe fittings. We also used them at the access, but they were slightly slanted and put on loosely. They are held in their lowest position via two round head screws. In order to flip up the cushioned center tube, which serves as a backrest, both fittings need to be pushed to the top. While doing that, they spread apart due to the angle and reveal the end which is clipped in (the other end is screwed tight). While closed, secure the open side with a splint.

HERMANN BOEHM, 53797 LOHMAR

GETTING ON BOARD COMFORTABLY

When mooring at floating jetties and skerries, it helps to have a bow ladder. Conventional solutions have the disadvantage of having to be taken out of the locker to be placed at the bow pulpit. However, this bow step is always ready for use. Depending on the height, it can be used while folded as one step or lowered down as two steps. The step consists of two quarter-inch-thick, stainless-steel pieces and is screwed to the anchor fitting. The upper metal section is bent so as not to interfere with the anchor. A bolt is welded to the lower section. Now the second pivoting metal section is fitted and the upper step is welded onto the bolt, which does not pivot. Put anti-slip tape on both steps and you are done.

SEEN AT THE PORT OF ELLOES/SWEDEN

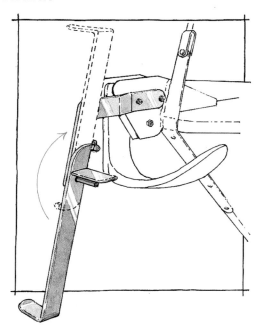

STEPPING SAFELY ON BOARD FROM THE ANCHOR

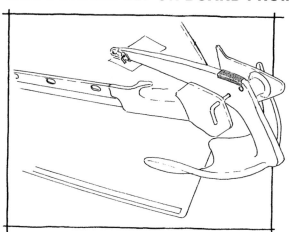

If you are mooring at a floating jetty, there is often the problem of having to take a big step to get on board. Not everybody wants to buy a bow ladder. To facilitate getting on and off the boat we have added a quarter-inch bolt with its respective drilled hole to secure the shaft. Now it can be used as a step. In order not to slip from the shaft when wet, we added a strip of waterproof, 40-grit sandpaper and glued it on.

ELKE HARMS, 24159 KIEL

BOW LADDER FOR LATERAL ENTRY

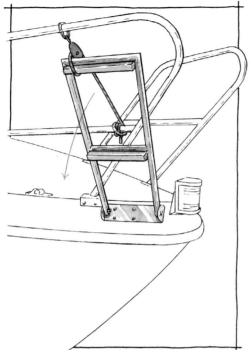

The higher the board of a boat, the more difficult it is to get on board, more so if you are mooring to a floating jetty. If you are at your own berth, you can get along fine with a fixed step, and when visiting foreign marinas, you may find overturned boxes and similar improvisations. However, a bow ladder is better and safer. They are available in many varieties, from simple wooden boards tied to the bow pulpit, to universal and telescoping stainless-steel ladders, to luxury solutions involving a folding step integrated into the anchor fitting (see Tips & Tricks in YACHT 23/07). Our somewhat unconventional ladder is not affixed to the bow pulpit, but right at the side of the hull, and it is easy to fold up with a pull line. It touches the bow pulpit without sticking out over it, so there is no interference with the sail or bow line or positioning lights. The particular advantage of this lateral ladder: if you moor on starboard, the boat can be placed with the bow to the pier, and you can use the ladder to get on board.

GERHARD KESSLER, 1218 GRAND-SACONNEX/ SWITZERLAND

RUBBER FOR ELIMINATING NOISE

If you regularly moor with the stern to the pier, you will eventually get yourself a gangway to step on land comfortably. Our gangway consists of a ladder with a sheet-metal insert that lies on the storage lockers, causing bothersome noises during choppy conditions. In order to save the boat's paint coat, and the crew's sleep, we needed a solution. It consists of two strong rubber slings that are tensioned between the sides of the stern railing and the legs of the ladder. When not stepped on, they lift the ladder a few inches from the deck. As soon as someone steps onto the gangway, it lies down safely on the deck.

PETER HAECKY, 4106 THERWIL/ SWITZERLAND

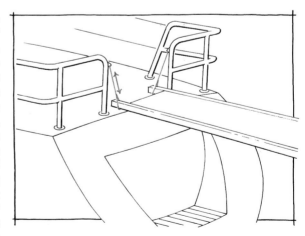

COCKPIT AWNING

While we yearn for the sun's radiation, it quickly becomes unbearable in midsummer. The solution is a sun sail hung over and across the cockpit. In order for the entire cockpit to be in the shade, it needs to be rather wide and its shrouds need to be tensioned. The stern usually does not provide enough fixation points. The boathook solves this problem. We tie it to the fixed mast support. Alternatively, use the backstay. This way you get nicely separated fixation points.

BERNHARD UHRMEISTER, BY EMAIL

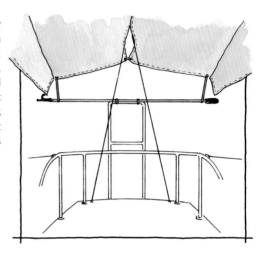

AWNING WITHOUT SAG

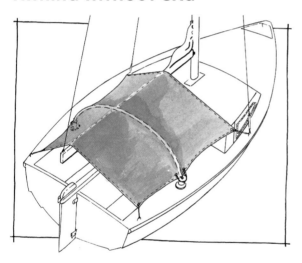

On sunny days we often run a rectangular awning over the main boom to provide shade, as many sailors do. We fix the corners closely to the deck. However, due to the low boom there isn't much space on our small Waarschip 570, and because the awning also sags quite a bit, we solved this inconvenience with a center spreader. We bought a fiberglass tent pole which we place over the boom and stick the ends into the openings of the winches, which happen to be at the right place on our boat.

WILFRIED KORFF, 40489 DUESSELDORF

SHELTER AGAINST THE WEATHER

You don't always have to completely cover the cockpit when you install a cockpit tent. With an additional section for the sprayhood, both the ladderway and the seats next to it can be effectively protected. Such an additional section does not require a frame, and zippers can be used to divide as required for the ladderway. The main advantage over a full tarpaulin: it can remain in place while sailing.

FRANK SCHAUWECKER, 23730 NEUSTADT

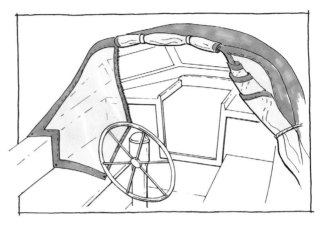

COCKPIT TENT FOR LITTLE MONEY

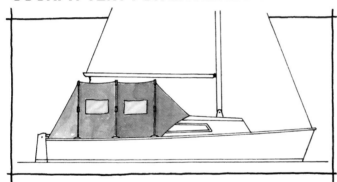

In order to save on storage space, we cut the poles in half and fitted them with plastic connectors, such as those used for cable tubing. We also used 90-degree sections for the roof poles. A rubber band inside of the poles prevents things from getting lost. The aluminum poles are threaded through the existing pole fittings and affixed to the Bimini mountings. To stabilize the construction, we tie it down at the mast and the engine fitting. The cockpit tent weighs less than 20 lbs., it can be set up and taken down in about ten minutes, and its size when taken down is only 30 x 8 x 8 inches. Overall, this modification has a cost of about 200 dollars and took one day's work.

FRANK VOLKMANN, 47443 MOERS

Our 15-foot dinghy cruiser offers only limited space. When you are traveling extensively, you need the cockpit as a living space. We happened to find a tunnel tent at an online auction (type Inca 3) that almost exactly matches the dimensions of the cockpit. With the exception of the floor poles, which we replaced with clip-on buckles, the tent was not modified. The poles for the cockpit tent consist of 20-mm aluminum tubes.

PIVOTING BATHING LADDER AT THE STERN PULPIT

Whenever a yacht is not moored to a jetty or quay—more so if its board is rather high—a swimming ladder is very useful to get from the dinghy to the cockpit. In the case of larger boats, they are usually at the transom. With my Hunter Pilot 27 this was not an option. For one, there is the rudder, which would be obstructed by a ladder. I also think that getting onboard from the stern during heavy weather is dangerous. A pilot ladder did not help much and lasted for one season only. I needed a stable ladder. The stern pulpit was the only place where it could be affixed. So, I built a step from stainless-steel tubes, which had a bend of about ten degrees at the lower section. Its shape follows that of the hull, against which it rests upon two short folding brackets. The ends of these small brackets are fitted with hardwood pieces so they do not scratch or damage the hull. The main trick consists of the two hinges, which were fitted to the stern pulpit tubes and angled at 45 degrees—the ladder swivels around these hinges into its horizontal position. While not in use it lies parallel to the railing wires. So, we eliminated the bothersome mounting and storing of the ladder. However, this does not work with all kinds of boats. If the angle of the stern pulpit is smaller or larger than 45 degrees, the ladder would be askew. To get on board comfortably, I replaced the railing wire to the stern pulpit with a snap line. This makes is possible to unlatch the railing with one move.

DAVID YOUNG, ENGLAND

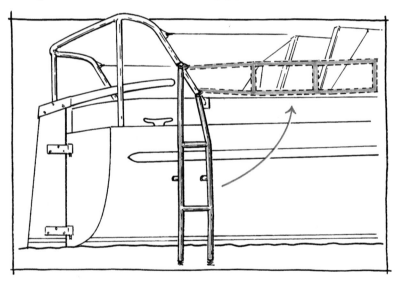

COCKPIT AWNING WITH A VIEW

A cockpit awning greatly raises the comfort level whenever you are sailing in colder climates. For one, you don't have to get into the cabin in case of an extended rain shower, and you can stay in the cockpit for some extra time after things get chilly in the evenings. In order not to have to sit in the dark, almost all cockpit awnings feature lateral windows. However, the view to the top is always obstructed by the awning. To change this we had an additional roof window fitted, and now we enjoy the increase of brightness and the great view of the skies. The much-improved luminosity makes for a higher quality experience, particularly when the days are grey. Even with our awning made of light-colored material, we've seen great improvement. If you have a darker awning, the change will be even more noticeable. So, far we have not had any problems with leaks at the seams.

THOMAS BOHLMANN, BY EMAIL

COCKPIT ROOF

Usually a sun roof placed over the main boom does not provide shade for the entire cockpit. We wanted to extend the UV protection to the stern and came up with the following system. We drilled a hole of about one-inch diameter into the boom head and inserted a short piece of plastic pipe used for electrical applications. Now we can put a nine-foot stainless-steel tube of almost an inch in diameter into the boom. The short section of plastic pipe prevents the stainless-steel tube from getting scratched and isolates both pieces of metal from each other. We also inserted hardwood sections

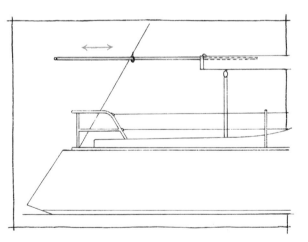

into the rear end and the center of the metal tube, both to make it more robust and to attach a spring eyelet—you need them to attach an awning. Then we added a stainless-steel ring to the backstay to hold the tube in place. To set up the awning we pull out the tube through the ring at the backstay and release the boom lift. The awning features a cutout for the backstay and now can be extended about three additional feet.

H. U. HEDINGER, 7502 BEVER/SWITZERLAND

CAMPING ATMOSPHERE IN THE COCKPIT

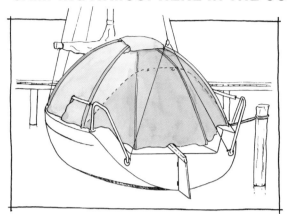

Small boats in particular offer only very little living space below deck, so a large cockpit is a much-welcome increase on board. Until now, I was discouraged by the high cost of custom-made awnings and tried to ignore the confined space. This year, however, I came up with the idea to modify a used dome tent as a cockpit awning. The best models are those where the outer and inner tent can be mounted separately and independently; if not, you would have to cut

out the tent floor. A two-to-three person tent is well-suited to cover the cockpit of a 22-foot yacht. The anchor points for the tent pegs are tied to the backstay and the bottom of the railway with rubber lines. Once you have moved the main boom out of the way, you are ready to set up the tent. In case you have to make any cuts or modifications, use a conventional sewing machine, which is suitable for this fairly thin fabric. Another advantage of a dome tent is its highly reduced packing volume. The fabric can be folded just as the lightweight poles.

Admittedly, the tent is not a very elegant solution, but whoever has tried it, even if just once at an uncrowded bay, will not want to forfeit the increased space again.

HAYO KOCH, 46537 DINSLAKEN

Editor's note: Even a beach shelter can provide a lot of comfort, as a minimalist cockpit tent or as a Bimini top.

AFFORDABLE BIMINI TOP

Many yachts in the Caribbean or the Mediterranean feature fixed awnings. This is not really necessary at our latitudes, but during midsummer and while at port, it is quite practical to have some shade. One of the very cheap solutions is a beach shelter. These mini tents are meant to protect from the wind and they can often be found on sale during summer. If you cut out the floor, you can also use them on board. Simply place the shelter onto the sprayhood and tie it down with a line, while at the back you can insert the fiberglass poles into the deck rim.

SEEN AT THE PORT OF TERSCHELLING

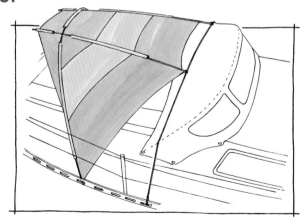

SPRAYHOOD HANDLEBAR

If you sail during heavy weather, you usually try to avoid getting onto the foreship. But there are times where you can't avoid it and you have to climb into it, so you should provide sufficient ways to secure yourself while doing so. The most critical moment might be when you step out of the cockpit onto the gunwale past the sprayhood. You could lock your safety line to the railing, but if you were to fall overboard you would be hanging helplessly from the boat's side.

A sturdy stainless-steel bar provides safety just like a handrail. It has been bolted to the deck and the cockpit using solid base plates and can be used by the crew in the cockpit as support, so many owners are outfitting their sprayhood with them. The handlebar even provides safety when the awning has been removed to have an unobstructed view—even

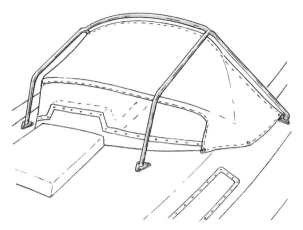

when a strong gale has ripped it away. In such a case, you can use the construction as provisional weather protection over the ladderway, which basically functions as a sprayhood.

SEEN AT THE YACHT PORT OF DAMP

EASY ACCESS TO THE BOW

Our 26-foot yacht was missing a handlebar on the sprayhood, needed in order to get to the mast or the foredeck without any danger. The next handle is available only after reaching the cockpit roof, which was not sufficient for us.

As our gunwale is not very wide, a solid handle from steel or aluminum would only lead to bruises, as you would constantly run against it. This is on top of the fact that such a bolted or welded solution would be considerably more expensive. So, I asked a sailmaker to add a solid fabric loop to each side of the cockpit awning. This solution has proven to be practical; it does not bother the gunwale and it was rather economical, too. Our sailmaker alerted us to the fact that the entire construction is only as firm as the fabric of the sprayhood, which is

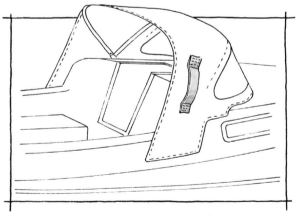

quite old and likely brittle, so there is a need to reinforce the inside to prevent the holding loop from ripping out and to provide a secure grip.

HARTMUT PITZKE, 31515 WUNSTORF

SPRAYHOOD WITH A GRIP

To provide additional support, we have added additional handrails for the cockpit awning. Weld a nut into the rounded ends. Drill a hole through the frame, and screw on the handrail from the inside. If you need to remove the awning, remove the handrail.

PETER F. MUELLER, 50858 COLOGNE

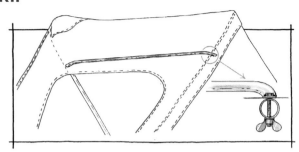

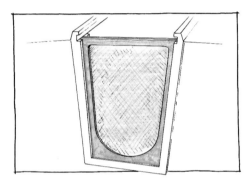

AIRY INSECT PROTECTION

If you leave the hatches and ladderway open during hot summer nights, to provide a breeze, there is the risk of a bug invasion. Because there are no stock mosquito screens, you need to make them yourself. The simplest solution is to glue together two simple plywood frames while inserting a mosquito fabric.

SIEGFRIED KLECK, 73760 OSTFILDERN

AIRY AND ROBUST SLIDING HATCH

Take a piece of fabric used for mosquito nets and sew in three transverse ledges so that the distance between the first and the second ledge matches the length of the sliding hatch, and the distance between ledges two and three matches its height. The advantage of this construction is that it can easily be adjusted to the different possible openings.

JAKOB GYARMATI, BY EMAIL

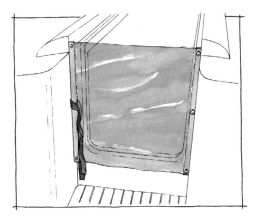

FLEXIBLE HATCH

While at port we replace our wooden hatch with a tonneau cover cut from sprayhood window foil. It is reinforced with vertical strips of self-adhesive cloth at its edges and held in place with three push buttons. When not in use, the foil is simply rolled to one side and secured with a piece of line.

SIEGFRIED DUSING, 21129 HAMBURG

SUPER NET FOR THE DECK HATCH

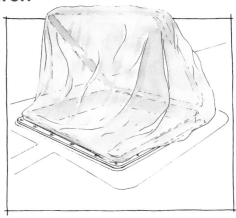

Mosquito nets for windows and hatches have their flaws; if they don't seal completely they offer only poor protection. However, the more accurately they are fitted to the shape of the opening, the more difficult it is to operate hatches and windows (e.g., in case of sudden rainfall).

We have found a surprisingly simple alternative, when compared to the solutions usually provided by the manufacturers, and have tried it successfully during summer: we used a net from a baby stroller (ours cost us about seven dollars) with an elastic band sewn into its perimeter. It fits the coaming of our foreship hatch exactly and keeps the net in place even with stronger winds. You might have to shorten the elastic band a little. The net itself is large enough that it even fits over the opened hatch. This means you can open and close the hatch from the inside without having to take off the protection.

VOLKER LUETKEWITTE, 33129 DELBRUECK

SHADE FOR THE FRONT HATCH

In order to keep the cabin cool, we have sewn fitting covers for the hatches from tarpaulin fabric. The edges were fitted with Velcro®. More Velcro® is affixed to the corresponding locations at the aluminum frame. These simple covers have proven their function for six summers in the Aegean Sea so far. They also protect the Plexiglas® from premature aging due to UV rays.

WOLFGANG HOFFMANN, 68542 HEDDESHEIM

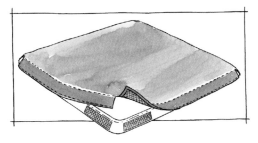

WATERTIGHT AND AFFORDABLE

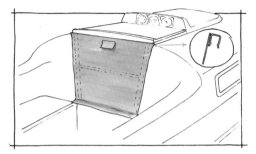

The hatch of our boat is not 100% watertight, so in case of heavy rain, we are using a tarpaulin made from garden pond fabric. Cut the foil to size and leave sufficient extra length. At its top we have glued a PVC cable guide that allows us to hang the tarpaulin onto the hatch. If necessary, add an opening for the lock and cover it with a piece of foil.

THOMAS BECKER, 44869 BOCHUM

VENTILATION WHILE IT RAINS

Yacht windows usually open towards the interior, so when it rains the water runs over the deck right into the boat. Our solution: we affixed a piping rail to the top of the window that deflects the rainwater. In addition, we made an awning with piping rail fitted to the size of the windows that can be tightened with rubber slings. This makes it possible to ventilate while it's raining, and even if there are unexpected nighttime showers, the bunks stay dry. Piping rail can be purchased at a sailmakers' or camping equipment suppliers.

WOLFGANG SZULZEWSKI, 38471 RUEHEN

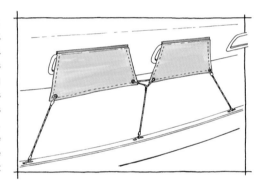

DECKCHAIR FOR THE LADDERWAY

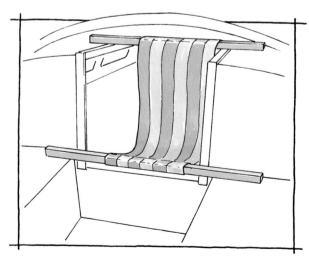

The best place on our Folke boat is our special deckchair, which we use while at port or while anchoring. It consists of only two ledges, which have to be long enough so that they don't slip into the ladderway. The fabric for the seat came from a conventional deckchair. Depending on the local conditions, the ledges can be fitted with rubber rings to avoid slippage. The position of the deckchair is protected from the wind and has a great view of the stern section.

ANDREAS REICHERT, BY EMAIL

BETTER SEATING

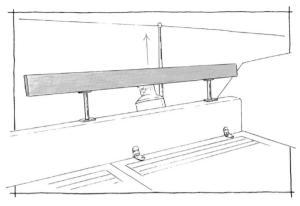

The cockpit coaming of our boat is pretty low. While this is visually appealing, the seating comfort is limited, as you cannot lean back comfortably. To provide a solution while at port we have developed removable back rests. Two oarlock fittings are inserted into the coaming, and two strong stainless-steel supports are made to fit into them. A teak board fitted with oarlocks serves as a backrest.

FRED SOMMER, 22523 HAMBURG

HEAT STORAGE

With respect to heating for small boats, many solutions have been provided over time. Due to a possible lack of oxygen, an open gas flame is not entirely safe, but it is still the most simple solution if sufficient ventilation is provided. We use a hearth stone or fire brick as heat storage—they are available in several sizes at low cost. Once it has cooled down a little, we place it onto a wooden frame to keep food or beverages hot. And it can also be used as a warming "bottle" when placed into a bag made of cloth to keep your feet warm.

DIETER BONDZUS, 24159 KIEL

STANDING ROOM FOR THE HELMSMAN

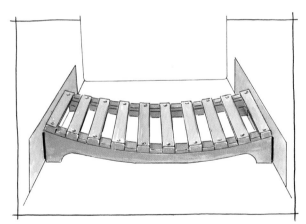

In order to stand comfortably at the helm with list, we have built a curved rack from robust wood. As the radius of the curve matches my inseam I can stand upright. The rack is fixed to the trapezoid-shaped cockpit by pinning it to the walls. Foam rubber strips at the four edges of the rack and thin stainless-steel sheets, which we have glued to the cockpit walls, protect the gel coat from scratches.

KARL-HEINZ TEINERT, 22927 GROSSHANSDORF

INCLINED PLANE FOR THE HELMSMAN

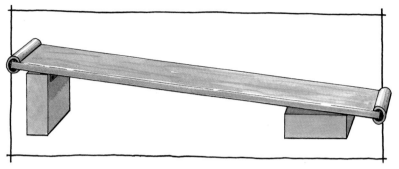

The sprayhood of our boat is such that smaller persons cannot see past it when steering while standing, which is usually preferred. Usually only a few more inches are all that is required. This has given me the idea to develop a variable pedestal. It consists of a sturdy board (about half-an-inch thick) that fits in nicely between the lateral walls of our cockpit. I mounted two hinged supports, which raises the platform for the helmsman in two steps, and it is also easy to store away due to the hinged blocks. Another application: whenever we sail for prolonged periods of time with a listing boat, we simply flip one of the supporting blocks and get a tilted plane, which makes up for the list in most cases. This takes away the stress from the ankles and increases the stability of the helmsman during heavy weather.

ANDRI DEN DRIJVER, 47445 MOERS

BETTER COOLING

On most vessels the compressor units and heat exchangers of the cooler are placed in cramped and badly ventilated locations. If the heat exchanger is already fitted with a fan, the heat exchange usually works quite well. If not, it is advisable to mount a fan; it helps to reduce the runtime of the unit. You can optimize the energy savings by adding a temperature-controlled fan (from electronics retailers), which automatically removes more heat by spinning faster when the temperature increases.

TORSTEN KEIL, 34363 HOLTSEE

FLOOR HEATING

Despite having a heater, whether a fan or a fixed system, our salon tended to be rather unpleasant during early spring or autumn. The ceiling was too hot, but we had cold feet. You can't reverse the laws of physics, and due to our age, yoga postures with headstands were out of the question. We discovered that whatever works in bed may work on the floor and got ourselves a heating blanket.

In the evenings, while sitting at the salon table, we place the blanket on the floor and enjoy the comfort of nicely warm feet with the additional advantage of not having to set the heating so high.

WILLI NICKEL, 13187 BERLIN

FLOOR HEATING AND STEP, ALL IN ONE

Even after fitting a heater on board, it is not always possible to avoid cold feet—warm air rises up, it is as simple as that. So, we have built ourselves an effective foot heater from the most basic materials.

Take a robust wooden box with dimensions of roughly 12 x 16 inches and a height of about 8 inches, with a drawer-like floor, and insert an additional board with circular cutouts for two to three tealights. The top and the sides are fitted with several holes to allow for air circulation. The top board is protected against the heat with a sheet of copper, which is adapted to the box. This is important, as it tends to turn black really quickly. We have found that one single tealight is sufficient to provide for warm feet. We also use the box as a step next to the mast.

HEINZ HAMANN, 21709 DUEDENBUETTEL

ANCHOR BALL MOUNTING

If you use a headsail winch, then chances are you leave the sheet attached. We use the V-shaped space formed by the separating lines to place the anchor ball. Simply add two carabiners and hook them between the sheets whenever required. For it not to twist with strong wind, we have added some weight to the bottom by tying a line to it. This can also be used to tie the anchor light to it.

FRIEDER ROESSLER, 1166 PERROY/SWITZERLAND

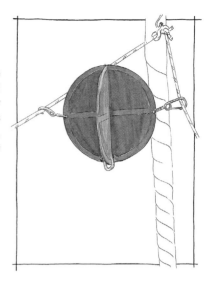

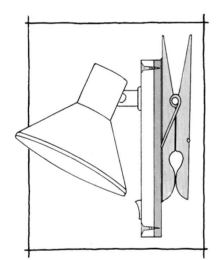

MOBILE READING LAMP

Who doesn't like to sit in the cockpit at night in candle light or the warm glow of a petroleum lamp? A nice idea, but these light sources are not really bright and hardly serve for reading a book. So, we got ourselves a 12-volt halogen spotlight from a camping supply store—a top-set model with an integrated switch. We mounted it onto a piece of plywood, to which we glued a wooden clothespin. Just run a cable to a 12-V source and clip it onto the sprayhood.

STEPHEN SPEIGHT, 24395 STANGHECK

GETTING HOT FASTER

We anchor quite often and have found that the 20-liter hot water boiler runs out too quickly. So, we have to run our Volvo MD 2020 a lot to get hot water. However, it takes about half an hour for the cold engine to reach the required temperature. (It doesn't help to raise the idling rpm, either.) But this changed rapidly when we tried this process with the reverse gear enabled. The engine quickly heats up when there is a load; it only took ten minutes to get hot water. The reverse gear has no influence on the anchor's hold.

HAUKE SCHMIDT, 24107 STAMPE

WELL HIDDEN: BOWSPRIT FOR BLISTER

The blister and gennaker develop their full potential the more out of the way they are of the main sheet. It helps to either add a bowsprit or a special feature at the spi boom, but we wanted to keep things simple on our touring yacht. It is far more simple and effective to affix a sturdy sprit below the anchor fitting or anchor roll. If necessary, flip it from its position so it lies horizontally. A firm bolt and nut hold the 15-inch long sprit in its position. If it is not in use, simply flip it out of the way. While planning and building the sprit, keep in mind that even a light wind will cause a significant shearing load.

DIETER BONDZUS, 24159 KIEL

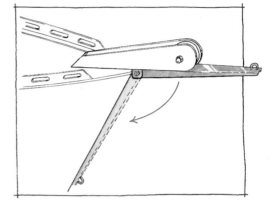

HOOKED FENDER

Every touring sailor knows this problem: when you are in a foreign port you never know where the vacant spaces are located. Just before entering a port, all the fenders are put out, just to find out later that it would have been better to put them further astern or even all of them on one side. So, all of the knots have to be untied and re-tied again at their new locations. This can turn into stressful port maneuvers, especially if you sail alone or with inexperienced passengers.

This is why we have added a plastic hook to the line about a foot from the fender. This makes it possible to quickly change their position at the right time. Once the boat is securely moored, the fenders can be tied down with the remaining line.

This method has also proven to work well when lying at port for some extended time. If the weather gets heavy, the fender is secured twice, thanks to the hook and the line. Some of our sailor friends liked our idea so much that they started re-fitting their fenders the next day.

ANDREA KOWALESKI, 30383 LOS NIETOS/SPAIN

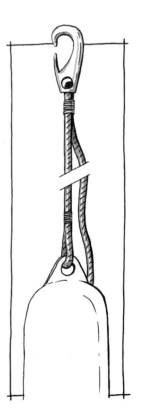

BETTER FOCUS WITH COMPASS GLASSES

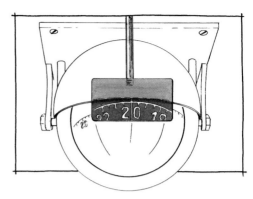

Our compass is quite far away from the cockpit. We almost need binoculars to check the position because it is mounted on the wheelhouse ceiling. We didn't want to add another compass, so the idea was to improve the readability of the existing one. I bought a standard rectangular reading glass of about 2 x 3 inches and removed the lens from its frame. To keep injuries to a minimum, it is best to choose a plastic lens. I drilled a thread into the center of its upper edge and added a thin stainless-steel rod with a matching thread. The other end of the rod is affixed to the ceiling with a clamp. This mounted magnifying glass makes it a lot easier to read the compass.
HEINZ HAMANN, 21709 DUEDENBUETTEL

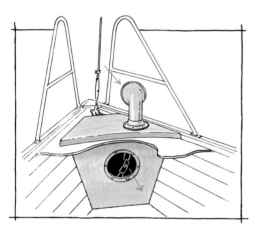

FRESH AIR OR ANCHOR AROMA

Small boats often have poor continuous ventilation. In order to improve the air circulation we fitted the anchor box with an air intake and added a watertight inspection hatch to the bow. While at port or anchoring, we open the hatch and the air circulates. You have to keep the anchor clean or you will smell it in your cabin.
JOCHEN PESCHKE, 22605

ELIMINATING NOISE

Once a wave hits the flat lower stern, you can pretty much forget about a quiet night in the stern cabin. A very effective device for minimizing noise can be manufactured with a piece of closed-cell foam, cut to match the stern waterline, which you then pull under the hull and secure there with two lines.
HELMUT GEBAUER, 24850 SCHUBY

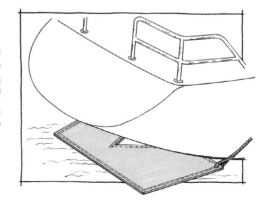

MORE ORDER FOR NAVIGATION

Most yachts tend to accumulate all sorts of riffraff on the chart table. This is particularly bothersome when you want to pull out a chart quickly or place it onto the table. To establish more order we bought a pair of solid wooden boxes that closely match teak or mahogany in color and are also moisture resistant. We have affixed them about two inches above the navigation table to the rear wall. Charts still fit under the boxes.

STEFFEN STANKE, 26121 OLDENBURG

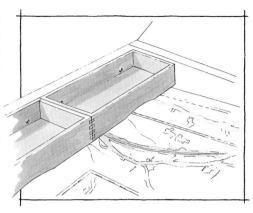

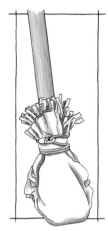

DIAPER CLEANING MOP

There have been prior tips as to how to soak up water using diapers. We place the diaper around a cleaning rag or mop and secure it with a piece of line, so we don't even have to bend over. Furthermore—and this is actually the main trick—we now reach the furthest corner of our deep bilge. We just leave it there for a moment while it absorbs the last drops of water. A large pack of diapers is not very expensive and lasts for the entire season.

STEPHAN JURCZOK, 13595 BERLIN

QUIET ON BOARD

Noisy floorboards are a nuisance and not conducive to good sleep, even if you sand them down so they don't touch each other. The noise comes from some area where they touch the base. If you screw them into the frame, you take away valuable storage space in the bilge, particularly in the case of small boats. We fitted all of the contact surface areas with self-adhesive sealing tape for window frames, leaving spaces so as to clean them easily. No more annoying noises! And we don't have to varnish the scratched frame that often anymore. You can find self-adhesive tape at a building supplies retailer.

TIM KRUG, 24159 KIEL

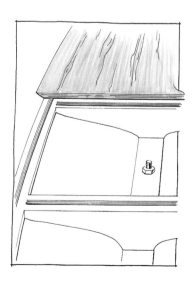

DECK LAYOUT & HANDLING

CHANGING THE TOW POINT

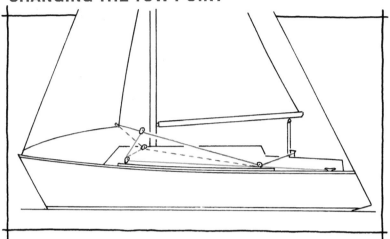

Until recently, we had to climb onto the gunwale after reefing the genoa in order to change the tow point, as our boat does not have a line-adjustable slider. With the following system you can run it from the cockpit: place a genoa slider close to the bow. Run a line with a thimble at its end through it. The sheet runs through the thimble and the rear slider. Tensioning the line changes the position of the tow point.

ROLF G. LANGE, 26919 BRAKE

ADJUSTABLE SHEET WAGON

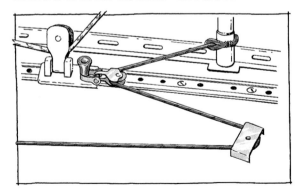

In the case of small boats you can adjust the sheet wagon with leading blocks even without a ball-bearing system. Place a flat line under the stopper button to disable it and run the line through a leading block towards the stern. You need to take off some pressure from the sheet before you can make an adjustment.

JOHANN KLEINRATH, 2823 PITTEN/ AUSTRIA

RIP LINE TO TAKE IN THE SPI

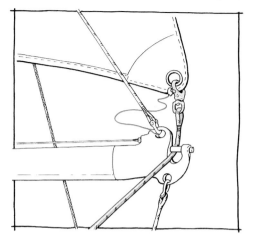

Many sailors, particularly regatta crews, still don't like to use a spinnaker sock. But when the family crew goes on a vacation outing, the spinnaker is often left in the sack out of respect for suddenly increasing winds or sudden gusts. Before the spi can be taken in, someone needs to go to the bow to release the spi guy. This maneuver can be eliminated by providing a small rip line. Snap a 3- to 4-foot-long line to the sail and latch the other end to the spi boom. When the sail needs to be hauled in, veer out the spi guy until the boom touches the forestay. If you keep veering the spi guy, the rip line tightens and opens the sheet shackle. Now the spinnaker can blow out and be hauled in below the main boom.

FRIDTJOF GUNKEL, 20251 HAMBURG

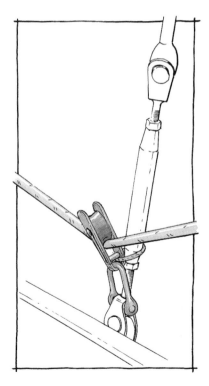

MORE EFFICIENT SHEET GUIDE

For many years we have used a self-tacking jib with our Rasmus 35 by Hallberg-Rassy, and our small crew as the standard headsail. It has been proven to be very practical when we encounter choppy waters and dense traffic. The only disadvantage: as has been described in previous *Yacht* issues, the boat does not sit too well with free wind and cannot provide the best possible propulsion. We have therefore provided additional tow points at the outer edge of the hull by latching a guiding block to each of the lower tensioners of the stern lower shrouds. We use it to reeve additional sheets that we change according to our needs. The self-tacking jib works much better now with free winds, and the boat is also noticeably more level. In case of strong winds in which we only run the jib we don't have to pole out the sail.

HERMANN HOYER, 22559 HAMBURG

LYING TO WITH THE SELF-TACKING JIB

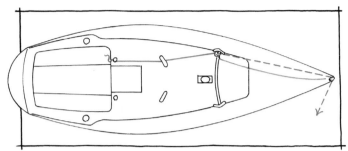

The advantages of a self-tacking jib are obvious and they make single-handed sailing a lot easier. However, there is one disadvantage related to single-handed sailing that should not be underestimated: heaving to with immediate lying to is not possible anymore, because the sheet cannot be reset with the slider. But the solution for this problem is actually very simple: I have tied an additional line to the sheet slider and tied it to an empty cleat on the cabin roof via a guiding block fastened to one of the two retaining brackets. If, just before lying to, you do not want to fasten the block at the corresponding side, then you better set up this system both at the starboard and port sides, although it is possible to change the setup on the fly.

If you haul this line tight, the self-tacking jib remains set back. If you want to continue sailing, release the auxiliary sheet. I have also chosen a long line, so it serves another purpose with free wind courses: it just takes one move to change its function from the auxiliary sheet to the gennaker neckline. I tie the front end at the sheet slider and take it to the bow past an additional guiding block at the bow fitting. This additional function allows for the often, only sparsely, available cleats to be used effectively.

TILL O. FLEISCHER, 79730 MURG-NIEDERHOF

EASYGOING FORESHEET

If you don't want to tow the dinghy, the only alternative is usually to put it on the foredeck with the bow facing forward, so the two lateral air chambers with the pointy ends are port and

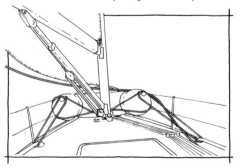

starboard of the mast. So, far, so good—the real problems show up when doing maneuvers. It happens quite often that the leeward genoa gets snagged at these pointy ends and the maneuver can be completed only after a crew member has cleared the sheet. This is not only awkward but also dangerous in case of strong winds. To fix this problem, we have added a line to the left and right of the regular dinghy lashing and guided them over the ends of the air chambers, tying them to the bottom railing. This prevents the slackened genoa from becoming stuck and the maneuvers turn out to be free of problems.

HANS-JUERGEN AMANN, 94327 BOGEN

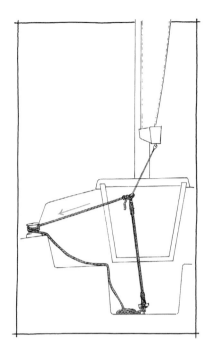

TRAVELLER REPLACEMENT

Boats without a traveller present the problem that, with little wind, the boom cannot be centered without the lower leech closing—the vertical force of the main sheet is too big. So, we apply the following method when there is only little wind: the line of the sheet is tied to the top main sheet block, and the line is tightened using the free windward side winch. We veer the sheet until the twist and angle of the sail are perfect. This way we get the same benefits of a traveller without having to deal with its disadvantages, such as taking up space, as well as the cost.

DIETER BEHRENS, 30655 HANNOVER

MINI FORESTAY SECURES JIB HANKS HEADSAIL

We use our headsail with conventional jib hanks. If there is a change of sail required, we lash the unused genoa to the railing. However, when there is a strong wind and high waves, the headsail is quickly washed astern. In order to avoid this, we have fitted a steel sling on either side of the bow pulpit. When we change sails, the jib hanks of the old sail are fastened to the leeside sling; shackling every other jib hank is sufficient. This keeps the sail in place during the change and you avoid having to tie it down all the way.

FRED SOMMER, 22523 HAMBURG

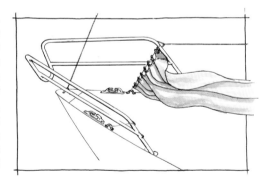

LASHED WITH ONE MOVE

We run the headsails with conventional hanks. The disadvantage is that the genoa needs to be lashed to the deck after hauling it in. To better lash the long sail, we came up with the following construction: two elastic lines are tied to the railing, as shown, and connected to a thin fiberglass rod with a plastic hook at its center. The rod is hooked to the railing and the lines hold the sails at the front and back.

HEINZ DIETER JUNGE, 24837 SCHLESWIG

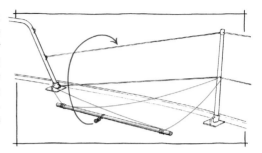

SAFER WITH A REMOTE RELEASE

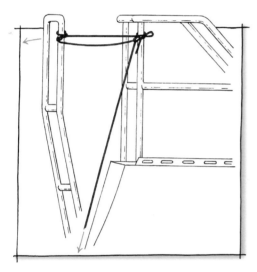

If you are in the water, the ladder is the best and often the only way to get back on board. Of course this only works if it's lowered; there are many boats whose stern ladder cannot be reached from the water. Sometimes it is tied to the stern pulpit so it does not fold down inadvertently, which is the case with our own boat. To be able to release the ladder for someone who goes overboard, we use the system shown in the drawing. We run a long line and tie it to the ladder so that the short end reaches the stern pulpit, where it is tied with a loose knot. The long end is also tied to the stern pulpit and threaded through a loop of the knot. This release line should be about one foot above the waterline. A strong pull at the line releases the loose knot at the stern pulpit, and the ladder swings downward.

VINZENZ SCHIMPFLE, 72285 PFALZGRAFENWEILER

TILLER RELEASE

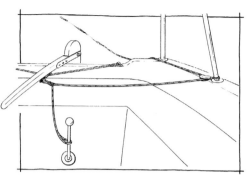

Small boats often do not have autopilot, so the rudder is sometimes locked. Many boats with well-trimmed sails stay on course rather well. If you are sailing by yourself, you will definitely appreciate this fact. However, what to do when you are not wearing a life belt, during calm weather, and you trip and go overboard? So, we added an eyelet to the eccentric clamp, or the rudder lock, and threaded an approximately 60-foot-long floating line to it. It runs through the stern pulpit and drags behind the boat. Doing between three and four knots, the person in the water has enough time to hold onto the line. The pull at the line releases the lock, and the rudder swings all the way to one side. We put the other end of the line over the accelerator to prevent the line from inadvertently getting into the propeller.

WERNER A. SUTTER, 4102 BININGEN/SWITZERLAND

KNOT RELEASE

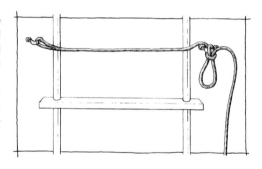

For safety reasons, stern ladders should have a release mechanism so they can be lowered from the water. Our ladder tends to move around with heavy seas, which is why we have secured it with a line. In order to release it from the water, we have added two fender eyelets, tied the line to one side, and then stretched it across the ladder. The trick is to tie a slipknot at the other side. We have a line that is long enough to reach the lower edge of the stern, so the ladder can be released with one pull and falls down.

ARRIEN TIEMON, 88677 MARKDORF

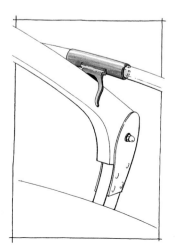

QUICK LOCK

I always sail my Marieholm 26 single-handed. In order to let go of the tiller for a moment, without engaging the autopilot, I needed a tiller lock that could be used quickly and with only one hand. The best solution is a mechanism I came up with, which is a plastic tube cut to the appropriate length with an added fork clamp, which is pinned to the crossbar of the stern pulpit. The folding tiller is easy to lock with an upward pull.

DIETER JUNGE, 24837 SCHLESWIG

TILLER LOCK

I often sail single-handed and for a long time I've looked for a simple solution to locking the tiller. The commercially available solutions seemed to me to be either too elaborate, too expensive, or too dangerous, due to sharp metal profiles. The best solution was a double-cleat (model CL 202), which I screwed flat onto the top side of the tiller. Both ends of the line running through the cleat are tied to the railing footer. By simply pulling at the central loop the tiller can be locked at any position. Cost: about 20 dollars.

HANS-GEORG CORDES, 30900 WEDEMARK

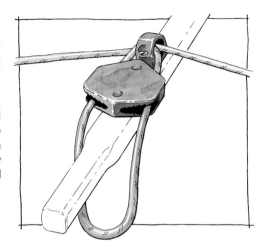

TAKING OFF THE EDGE OF CLEATS

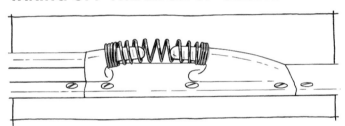

Cleats are practical for holding the lines at the right angle, at the right place. But they also tend to snag all kinds of lines at the worst possible time. No matter how skillful you are, in most cases, when trying to release the tangled line you will have to get there yourself to release it. This is a nuisance, more so while you are doing sports sailing or during a regatta.

You can get rid of this problem by cutting up a short piece of hose lengthwise and placing it over both cleats. However, a stainless-steel spring looks decidedly more elegant.

CHARLY LINNEMANN, PALMA DE MALLORCA/SPAIN

CONNECTORS BEHIND BARS

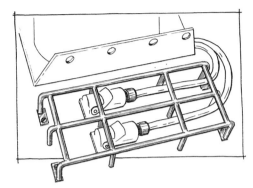

In most cases, the electric connectors of the power lines are right next to the mast step. But they are often in the way (e.g., when reefing the mainsail or flaking). Even if you are extra careful when close to the mast, at some point you will step onto them. Fixing broken connectors or lines is much more time consuming than fabricating a stable cage for the connectors ahead of time. For our boat, we welded a frame from stainless-steel rods that protects all the fragile electrical gear. We added four flat, stainless-steel pieces to the bottom of the cage where the protector is screwed to the deck. If necessary, you can remove the protecting cage without trouble (e.g., to remove the mast). The structure can take about 200 lbs., so even a forceful kick or step is not a problem. Lightweight passengers can use the frame as a step, for instance, to reach the mainsail.

HELMUT WENGLER, 14129 BERLIN

REDIRECTION TO AVOID MARKS ON THE GELCOAT

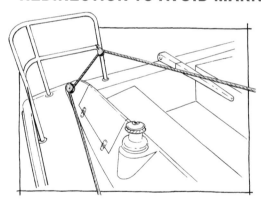

Unfortunately, even newer boats don't always have their fittings placed where they need to be while in use. This is particularly unnerving if it causes wear on the gelcoat, as is the case with our line for the headsail furling. Its guiding block is at the very edge of the slanted coaming, and whenever we stand in the cockpit and maneuver the headsail, the line touches the top edge of the storage locker lid and cuts deep scratches into the gelcoat. We prevent this from happening by stepping onto the gunwale when tightening the line, or we pull the line directly via the sheet winch. We only need the winch in case of very strong wind. To avoid damage and scratches while running the furling from the tiller, we simply tied a guiding block halfway up the stern pulpit. This prevents any chafing from pretty much any direction.

SIEGFRIED DUESING, 21129 HAMBURG

LEASHED MAINSHEET

Many touring yachts feature mainsheet systems, with travellers mounted on the cabin deck. However, the mainsheet at the boom's center makes for a shorter lever, which means that such systems require more effort and strength. If the tackle gets twisted and increases friction, you are faced with two problems: running the sheet is almost impossible; and simple clearing is out of the question, as you cannot reach the guiding blocks or pulleys from the cockpit, so someone else would have to climb up there. This used to happen onboard our yacht quite a lot. The standard blocks could not be locked, unfortunately. So, we drilled one small hole into each of the pulley's flanks and connected the two blocks at the boom with a thin line. Now they can't twist around anymore, and the mainsheet stays clear. We have traveled more than 1,000 miles with this method and not once did the tackle twist around. The sheet is now much easier to veer, particularly with light wind.

PETER F. MUELLER, 50858 COLOGNE

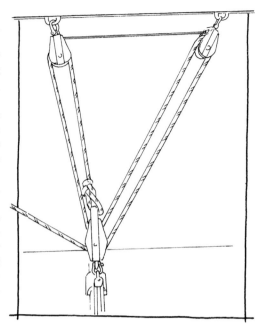

AID FOR THE MAINSHEET

As a single-handed sailor, I avoid leaving the cockpit during heavy weather. I have added a kicking strap to the main sheet so as to avoid having to go onto the deck of our Waarschip. Tie a thin line to the top of the sail; it will be raised when setting the sail. It is redirected via a block or pulley at the mast step towards the cockpit. To take in the sails, simply engage the lazy jacks from the stern and release the mainsheet. If the sail does not come down by itself, you can pull at the kicking strap until it is held by the lazy jacks and kept under control. I keep the kicking strap tight until I get into port. Once safely inside the box, the line is released and the sheet flaked.

WILFRIED KORFF, 40 489 DUESSELDORF

RUBBER TENSIONER

We use a conventional boom lift running from the boom head to the top of the mast and the mast step into the cockpit. As the leech of the mainsheet is loose, the line may get caught by the battens; it needs to be released before proceeding. In order to prevent the line from getting caught due to a loose boom lift, we have added a thin elastic rubber line of about 2.5 feet in length parallel to the boom lift. This way, the boom lift shortens automatically by about two feet and cannot become entangled anymore.
HANS-JOACHIM TREU, 82194 GROEBENZELL

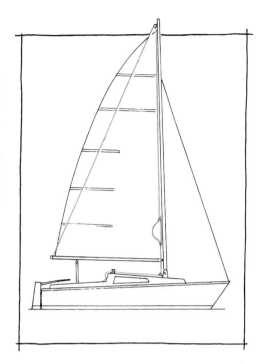

MOBILE TRAVELLER

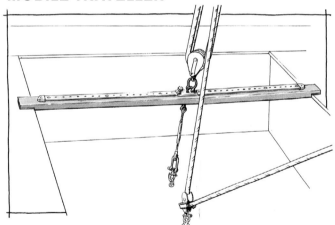

We went for a mobile traveller for our dinghy cruiser. In order to be able to continue using the storage lockers, we have mounted the traveller onto a sturdy mahogany ledge. It is fastened with a shroud tensioner and a snap shackle to the normal mainsheet anchor point at the cockpit floor. The block of the mainsheet is shackled to the traveller. To prevent scratches on the cockpit and slippage of the traveller, we glued rubber to the lower ends of the mahogany ledge. When we are in a port, it is easy to remove the construction to access the storage boxes.
WOLF-DIETER APITZ, 67354 ROEMERBERG

ORDER IN THE COCKPIT

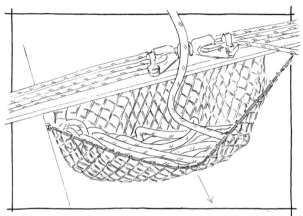

If you have lines all over the boat, they not only contribute to bad maneuvers, but they can also be quite dangerous. A loose mainsheet on the cockpit floor is easy to slip on, and it gets dirty and stays wet for a long time. Although there are line bags available for purchase, they have disadvantages: they are not exactly cheap; they are usually quite bulky; and a sheet that is kept in such a bag quickly gets musty because the net openings are usually rather small and do not allow enough air circulation. So, we have added a bag made from affordable railing net below the traveller. Add two or four fender eyelets below the rail by screwing them into it. A line holds the net via these eyelets. To put in and take out the lines we only keep a fixed line at the front; at the stern we use an elastic line. This makes is easy to open the net and keep things in the cockpit orderly. A wet sheet can dry pretty quickly as well.

BRIGITTE LANGE, BY EMAIL

WINCH HANDLE AS A TRIM HANDLE

Thin lines are rather difficult to tension by hand. Sometimes these lines are way too heavy for the purpose. In order to tension thin lines adequately, we have screwed a camcleat onto our winch handles where we can fasten lines. By holding the handle left and right of the cleat, we can put a lot more tension on the line. It is important that the holes are not drilled at the edge of the handle, or else there is the danger of it breaking under stress.

EIKE KOETHER, 28844 WEYHE

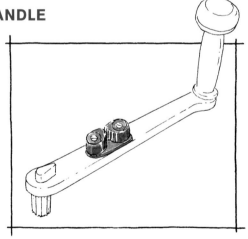

EASY STORAGE AND ALWAYS READY

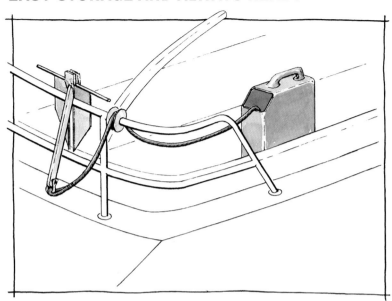

Where are you supposed to store the stern anchor gear? Even large yachts over 30 feet rarely feature a fixed solution, less often for smaller boats. If you own a 28-footer, like we do, and you are sailing in the Mediterranean, where you have to work a lot with your stern anchor, then you have to come up with a solution. We actually prefer to do the Roman-Catholic anchoring with the bow forwards. There are several advantages to this: we don't have to walk across a narrow and unstable board; we use our sturdy bow ladder to get on land instead. Furthermore, underwater obstacles do not pose a risk to the stern and the fragile rudder during a swell.

The anchor itself has its fixed position at the stern pulpit, where it is tied down, but there is not sufficient space for the chain forerun and anchor line. So, we had to find a place where both would be handy and their use wouldn't involve a lot of handling of lines. Also, 30 feet of chain forerun and 90 feet of line add up to quite a lot of weight that we did not want to have around at the stern.

After several experiments involving cloth bags, buckets, and other containers we chose a plastic jerrican, which is large enough to store everything, including the loose anchor line. We don't have to coil it up, we just feed it hand over hand through the opening. This makes it easy for it not to get entangled when setting the anchor. The chain forerun is placed on top of it. We cut the plastic jerrican so that the grip remained intact, while the opening for the line is rather small and high up, which prevents its content from spilling out when it's full and tips over. Our mobile anchor box is stored in the locker under the thwart.

BERT HAGER, PER EMAIL

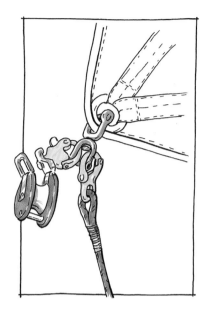

BOWSPRIT REPLACEMENT

To optimize the performance of our 41-foot sloop, we have bought both a spi and a blister. As a bowsprit, we use the existing spi boom and affix it to the deck using the spi fitting. We take it off the mast track and use the threaded bolt to affix it to the cover of the chain plate. The boom is actually able to telescope and reaches some three feet out over the bow fitting. Even though it is lashed to the side of the bottom railing, its fitting is exactly in the center line of the boat.

KONRAD RINGLER, 76887 BERGZABERN

CONTROL ROLL

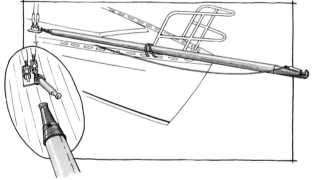

The profile of blisters and other light sails is best controlled via a tripping line at the luff. The tack of the sail should be able to move up and down the stay. If you hook it with a shackle directly to the cable, you will get rather loud buzzing noises. They can be minimized with a snatch block.

GERHARD KESSLER, 1218 GRAND-SACONNEX/SWITZERLAND

CLEVER SPLINT LOCK

To make sure that nothing gets snagged in the splints of our splint tensioners, we covered them with shrink hoses. This insulation material that shrinks when heat is applied can be purchased at electronics retailers (large diameters are also available). About 38 mm is sufficient for the splint tensioners used on 30-foot yachts. When rigging up, we push short sections over the tensioners. After the rig has been trimmed, we use a hot air blower to heat the hoses that cover the toggles and splints.

DIETER BEHRENS, 30655 HANNOVER

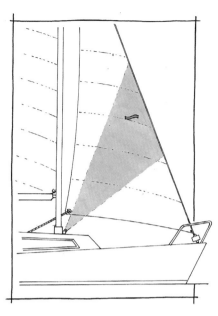

PERFECT TRIM AT NIGHT

When competing in regattas, it is important to trim the sails perfectly during the night. We added an LED flashlight to the front mast step so that the helmsman doesn't have to use his white flashlight all the time to follow the telltales. To minimize the glare, we simply glued some yellow foil to its front. We used cable ties to affix the light at the mast step so that the light beam catches the genoa telltales.

WERNER FRIE, BY EMAIL

WITHOUT KINKS

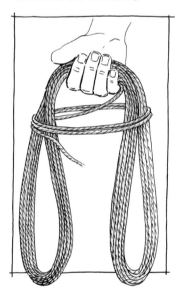

As a sailing mountaineer, I wonder why so many yachtsmen choose to tolerate the kinks they create when coiling up their lines. Unfortunately, the "correct coiling" of a line is still taught with the famous right-hand spin for every length of the line. Certainly a coiled line with parallel loops looks a lot better than a bunch where figure eights and loops mix with each other. But the advantage is that this coil can be opened and spooled without any kinks in the line.

Among mountaineers, the so-called lap-coiling method has proven to be efficient and practical. We don't place the loops in a row next to each other, but rather they are placed as long loops running from one side to the other, which meet where the hand is holding them. Due to the alternating direction there is no continuous twist in the line, and so it can be extended without forming kinks. With some practice and care, you will quickly make clean loops, so the visual aspect is not left behind. The final step, as usual, is several horizontal round loops that hold the two halves of the loop tightly at the center. There are several ways to tie up the loops of the line, depending on your preference. Make sure that you tie up the line so the end does not get loose inadvertently.

SAM ACKERMANN, 3014 BERNE/SWITZERLAND

MOBILE SPRING CLEATS

Spring cleats mounted at the center of the gunwale are very helpful for safely mooring the yacht. Unfortunately they are becoming rare, as many boatbuilders do not include them because of cost considerations. This is quite bothersome, because mounting them later on is an elaborate task. These cleats have to withstand considerable stress, so large base plates are required, and with sandwich decks it is necessary to replace the core material with a special method that includes laminate, or resin, and hardener in order to be absolutely waterproof and solid (see also YACHT 18/04, page 104). There are many yachts on which this is not possible because the relevant deck areas can only be reached by removing parts of the fittings or inner hull. In case you have a large and solid bolted railing you can add custom-shaped bases using bolts. Another solution consists of cleats that are placed onto the genoa rails using a slider. However, they are rather expensive and need to remain on the slider permanently, as they can only be removed after taking off the end sections. While sailing they tend to make things messy, as lines may get caught and you might trip over them.

We built two divisible cleat sliders from stainless steel which fit the profile of the genoa rail, and they can be taken apart lengthwise at about one third to two thirds of their width. Both sections of the slider are held together with a bolt with an Allen head. The cleat itself consists of solid, round stainless steel and has been welded to the broader section of the base. An additional bolt can be used to affix the cleat from above to the holes in the rail. When not in use, it can be removed quickly and does not interfere at all.

HEINZ HEGNER, 46236 BOTTROP

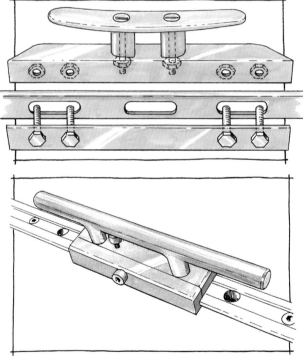

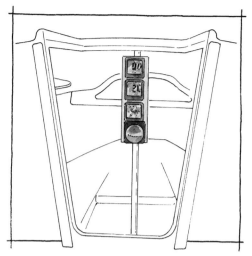

INSTRUMENT HOLDER

We have a Sunfast 20 and we definitely appreciate having information concerning wind direction and wind force, as well as water depth and speed. The only problem was inadequate space to put the instrument panels. We found some wooden boxes at a Swedish furniture retailer and mounted the instruments into these boxes and to the mast support, which happens to be in the back of the cabin. Now the helmsman can read the information with ease from his position.
HORST GEERS, 49413 DINKLAGE

MULTI-FUNCTION GPS CLAMP

If you've ever chartered a yacht, you may know the problem: unfamiliar navigation instruments and no idea how they work. Do you want to read the manuals? This could mean that vacation is over by the time the GPS works as you want it to, and it may well be that the manual is only available in the local language. So, the best solution is to bring along your own handheld GPS. Unfortunately, chartered boats usually don't feature an appropriate support. So, I built a simple and flexible GPS clamp for my Garmin GPS-72. I screwed the lower part of the GPS, which can be purchased as an original support, onto an aluminum plate (about 3 x 3 inches). Now I can attach different sets of clamps, which allows me to place a clamp onto almost any pipe diameter (e.g., at the steering wheel column, onto a handrail, and even the handle of the onboard bicycle mount).
LEO SCHMITZ, 33102 PADERBORN

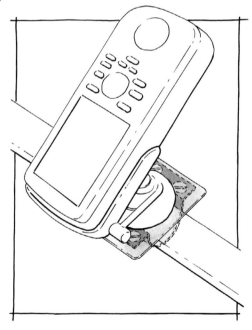

UNIVERSAL GRASPER FOR HALYARDS

Although this topic has been dealt with before, here is yet another tip for threading halyards through a clamp lever. We use a flexible grasper, which can be found at most building material retailers for a few dollars. Of course, this tool is helpful for many applications, for example, to get a lost screw from the most remote corner of the engine room or to grab a cable. The only disadvantage of these flexible helpers is that they are not rust-proof, so they age rather quickly.

WOLFGANG MAJDIC, 40724

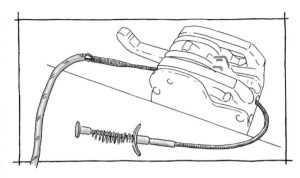

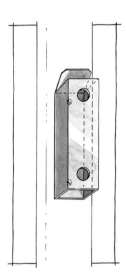

SHEATH FOR MULTITOOL

Most sailors need their pocket tool whenever it is not handy, so I added a receptacle for my knife above the mast step. I cut out three sides from the lower section of a square aluminum profile (approximately 2 x 3/4 x 4.5 inches) and bent the remaining one so that the knife cannot slip out. I mount the sheath with a counter plate and two screws inside the mast track.

EDGAR WALLENBORN, 50171 KERPEN

BOX FOR THE VENT

If you don't shift your vents leeward, it can rain right into the cabin. Absolute protection is provided by putting a bucket over the vent with its ventilation cutout facing the opposite direction.

MATHIAS BIMLER, 85354 FREISING

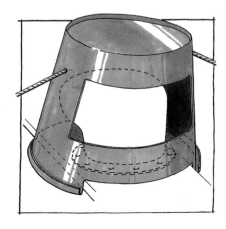

SAVING ENERGY

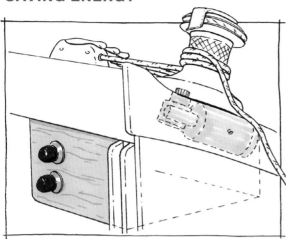

We have been sailing on Lake Constance with our Vindoe 40 for thirty years. At age 80, I have been on many trips all around the world and was able to log my personal experiences. I have no plans for throwing in the towel anytime soon, but unfortunately, sailors age like everybody else. Fading strength can, however, be compensated by technology in some instances. We would like to present one that may come handy for people with similar problems.

We think we should complement each other with the jobs at hand and be able to replace each other as much as possible, in case one of us suddenly finds himself or herself without any help. My wife found out that she could not raise the mainsheet using the winch next to the ladderway, so we had an electric winch installed. The controls were placed right next to the ladderway at the engine compartment. This power package has up to 550 lbs. of pulling force; we can pull all of the rerouted lines from the cockpit, including reef and auxiliary lines. If necessary, we can use the winch to push the sheets through by rerouting them to the electric winch on the coaming. When the wind gets too strong, we use the same method to bring up the anchor or maneuver at port if necessary. It can also be used to get aloft without help.

Another important function of the new winch is its safety feature. If one of us should go overboard, we can use pulleys and the electric winch. We suggest you test it out beforehand so you don't lose precious time trying to figure out how it works in an emergency.

CHRISTOPH WOCHER, 88085 LANGENARGEN

BOATHOOK FOR MULTIPLE USES

A boathook should serve several purposes: a small spinnaker fitting turns it into a pole, and the snap shackle in the middle spreads the awning.

JOHANN KLEINRATH, 2823 PITTEN/ AUSTRIA

SAFELY TO THE BOW

When you have to get to the foreship, the most critical place—once you leave the cockpit during heavy seas—is between the handrail on the sprayhood (if you happen to have one) and the handrail on the cabin. If you don't trust the railing with its give, or if the usual solutions are too expensive (see YACHT 22/04), simply add an additional handrail that reaches from the sprayhood to the deck.

HANS RICHTERS, 38446 WOLFSBURG

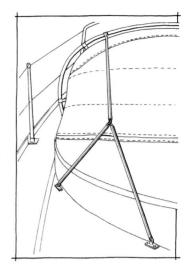

LINE HOLDER

Lines on deck are a considerable safety issue for the crew, both at sea and at port, as there is always the possibility of tripping over them and getting hurt. So, we always coil up all of the lines and hang them onto the railing or the mast. We use homemade slings with a spliced eye at one end of the line and a diamond knot at the other. The slings are easily opened and closed and can be placed anywhere using a clove hitch.

KARL BAREUTHER, 24960 GLUECKSBURG

ROPE BAG

Instead of coiling up lines, which always causes kinks and woolding, we put them into bags or buckets without twisting them. You must be careful so that both ends of the line are at hand. We place the lower end so that it sticks out at the top and secure the top end to it after filling the bag. This way the lines are always ready for use.

ERICH LAZARUS, 81373 MUNICH

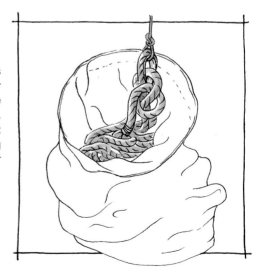

SUCTION HOLD

A siphon or vacuum lifting cup tool (for glass plates) is a great base for any fitting on a smooth surface, and it does not require drilling holes, or glue. I was looking for a way to add a sunshade for the cockpit of my Leisure 17 when sailing with stern winds. In order to attach the sunshade's pole to the base, I have mounted an aluminum tube using wingnuts.

HORST EHRLE, 88046 FRIEDRICHSHAFEN

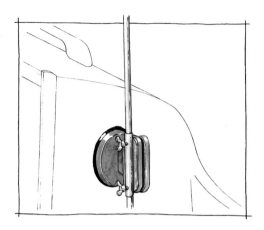

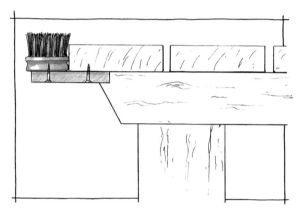

CLEAN FEET

Many port operators do not allow you to nail a floormat to the jetty. The reason: the mats trap the moisture and the wood of the jetty deteriorates much faster. I just got myself a scrubber and screwed it from below to the front of the jetty. Our solution works really well and actually looks a lot better.

HELLMUT KOCH, 38100 BRAUNSCHWEIG

CANVAS SHADE

The classic bent-board, or hatch, is quite bothersome and uncomfortable to handle, but required at port to provide privacy. To avoid waking up the crew while getting out at night, I have made a replacement from canvas. It is supported by two spars which are placed into the lateral guiding rails.

The canvas features two hemlines. When not in use, the screen is rolled up and stored in a cupboard.

DORIS TWARDZIOK, 25938 WYK AUF FOEHR

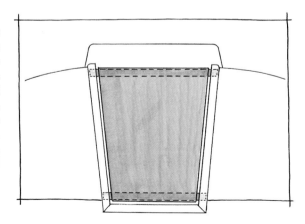

WINCH HOLDER

We sometimes use a fishfinder to choose the best anchoring place. Since we use the gear only occasionally, we did not want to drill any holes into the boat, nor did we want to have the included fixed baseplate in our cockpit. We also didn't like the other mounting options, like gluing or clamping. While looking for a flexible support we found a winch holder for sunshades. Although this construction was not usable for our purpose, it provided the initial idea. We cut off the arm of a low-priced aluminum winch crank and used a screw to mount the standard holder of the fishfinder to the arm. Now we can quickly place the echo sounder into the genoa or mainsail winch. The winch is secured with a locking mechanism so there is no danger of it going overboard. The entire mount cost about 25 dollars and it took about half an hour to build.

ROLF JUNGNISCHKE, 21465 REINBECK

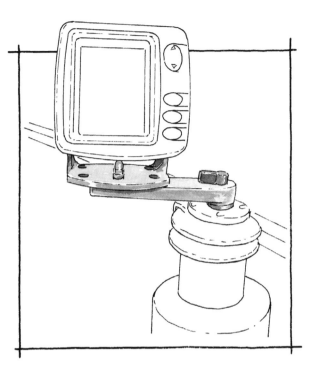

SIMPLE CHAFING PROTECTOR

Wind and water exert considerable stress on the tarpaulin during winter: the sections where it rests on the railing are particularly prone to chafing. To solve this inconvenience, we use heating insulation foam from a building supply retailer. The sturdy foam tubes can be used to cushion the bow and stern pulpits and the t-sections fit rather well to the railing supports. Due to the lateral slits, they are easy to fit.

GÜNTHER ERWIED, 80797 MUNICH

SIMPLE LINE SHACKLE

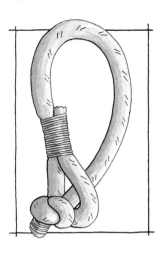

We use a piece of soft half-inch sheet line and make a figure eight knot at one end. The other end is folded into an eyelet and sewn tight. Fashion the diameter of the eyelet so that the knot barely slips through it. Under stress, the eyelet doesn't allow the knot to slip through. This shackle is not meant for supporting high loads, but it can be made without splicing ropes or complicated knots.
HEINRICH DAVATZ, 8800 THALWIL/SWITZERLAND

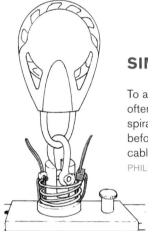

SIMPLE MOUNTING

To avoid jib pulleys or mainsheet blocks from banging around, they are often mounted with springs. However, it is not easy to place the steel spiral between the block and the padeye—the pulley often slips away before you can screw the shackle bolt in place. We fix the springs with cable ties so the mounting is easy and comfortable.
PHILINE PESCHKE, 22605 HAMBURG

SEAWORTHY SEAT

Sailing with small children requires special attention. If one parent takes care of the juniors, there is not a problem, but what happens when a maneuver requires all available hands on deck? We have modified a child's bicycle safety seat so that it can be placed close to the ladderway. We used plywood to rebuild the lower section of the bulkhead, and a piece of square aluminum profile is screwed to the top edge of the plywood. It has two holes that fit the two bolts of the seat. The children's seat can be set onto the aluminum profile, and the little sailor is safely secured. Because these seats are fitted with safety belts, the child can't "fall out of the saddle" either. Protected from the sun, wind and rain, our junior

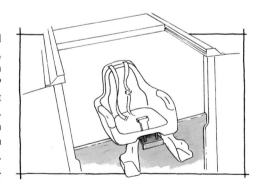

now has a front row seat with a direct view to his parents. The cockpit remains roomy and all of the maneuvers can be done without any problem.
SUSANNE RITTER-KETTENBACH, 65343 ELTVILLE

STEP PROTECTOR

Our X-119 has a simple aluminum profile for the bent-board (hatch). Due to stepping onto it continuously to enter the cabin, this profile had been damaged quite badly. In order to protect it, I added a teak ledge to the outer edge. I also added a water drain to the center of the ledge, as well as a piece of neoprene to protect the shins.

PETER HAECKY, 4106 THERWIL/
SWITZERLAND

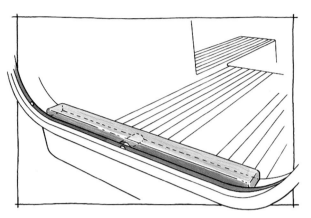

COMFORTABLE LADDERWAY

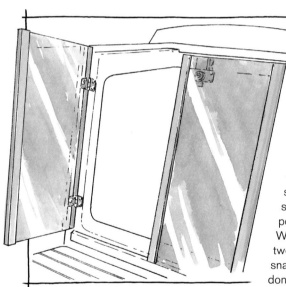

Since we are sailing fairly calm regions, the heavy and sharp-edged hatch is always bothersome. Every time you open it you ask yourself "where do I put it?" Whenever we leave the ship, we have to get the hatch from below the bunk. If we are not careful while handling the unwieldy acrylic hatch, we can also leave permanent marks on the interior finish. To make handling much easier, we cut the hatch at the center and framed both sections with teak ledges. The starboard side with the lock overlaps with the portside, so that both doors can be locked. We mounted the finished wing doors, with two hinges each, to the ladderway. Two snap locks keep the doors in place so they don't flap around. This suggestion makes sense only if your cockpit has space enough that the open doors are not in the way.

HERMANN BOEHM, 53797 LOHMAR

NAVIGATION DESK AT THE LADDERWAY

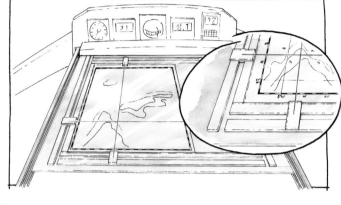

If you want to have a quick look at your charts, you usually have to go to your navigation corner in the cabin. My wife had the idea to add a transparent release made from tinted Plexiglas® to the hatch of our Compromiss 888, which made me develop this idea even further: because I had put my charts on the existing cover occasionally anyway, I soon arranged for the Plexiglas® hatch to be our new navigation center. So, I bought another clear Plexiglas® sheet and several 3/4- and 1-inch strips from the same material. I glued them at a right angle onto the tinted glass so that the clear sheet fits exactly into the center. Now the charts and maps are protected from spray and kinks and are always handy, and I don't have to go into the cabin anymore.

I also added a crosshairs, which makes it possible to mark locations on the map, by gluing the strips so that small Plexiglas® pieces can be moved along all four sides inside a groove.

I connected these pieces with a section of sewing elastic, which resulted in having the said crosshairs at my disposal. For better orientation, I glued paper strips with markings under the Plexiglas® pieces. I can set the crosshairs precisely, even when the mile-markers can't be seen on one of the edges.

Simply set the GPS coordinates with the crosshairs and you are ready to see your precise location. This is a lot faster than using traditional methods, like navigation triangles.

Another advantage: I can mark the course and any other data with a waterproof pen on the top Plexiglas® sheet and simply wash it off with alcohol when the trip is over.

KLAUS NITTEL, 46562 VOERDE

DAMPENED MAINSHEET

Sometimes the best ideas are lying at your feet. While looking for a cheap boom dampener, I found the easiest solution in a simple shock absorber, as it can be inserted into many lines, including ours and others'. I tied it to the mainsheet so it is always ready for action when sailing downwind courses. In the case of tackle systems, the shock absorber must be inserted with a line between the boom and the pulley. The shock absorber doesn't avoid accidental jibes, but it lessens the impact from the boom.

ARMAND U. MARIE-LOUISE ANDEREGGEN, 48400 BODRUM/TUERKEI

IMPROVED CRANK SUPPORT

Once again, the mainsheet has become entangled in the jib at the winch handle and has almost thrown the precious item overboard. To avoid this kind of scenario, we cut out the top edges of the support.

This is fairly easy to do with a sharp knife or a soldering iron. The crank now sits in its support with the handle safely tucked to the side.

EIKE KOETHER, 28844 WEYHE

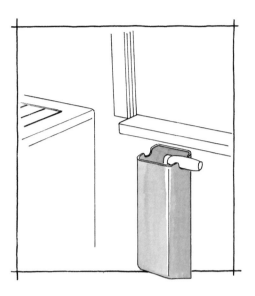

SIMPLE INSTRUMENT PROTECTION

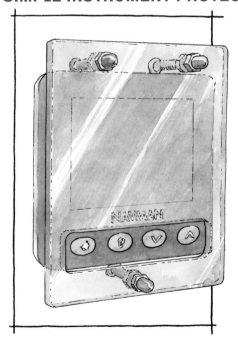

On sporting yachts with tiller steering, the instruments are usually mounted at the hatch next to the ladderway. When you are busy with maneuvers, they can easily get kicked or receive a blow. Displays are likely to crack, water gets inside, and the expensive piece of equipment is rendered useless. To prevent this from happening, we have fitted our X-79 with protective shields: we cut the Plexiglas, or Makrolon®/polycarbonate plates, so that they are slightly larger than the instrument's cases. At the top and bottom I put in three countersunk bolts with two nuts each, so that the nuts reach behind the case. At the front we use dome nuts to avoid sharp edges. The length of the bolts is determined by the depth of the instrument case. Of course, we deburred the edges and rounded the corners. Due to the cutout at the height of the buttons, the instruments can be used with the protective case mounted in front of them. Now our instruments are protected with a simple plate. If you are worried about getting scratched or bruised, place some rubber caps over the nuts. In case the protective shield cracks, we simply put the spare one we have in its place.

JENS KINZEL, 31832 SPRINGE

RIG & SAIL

TENSIONED LAZY JACKS

I have fitted my boat with a sail cover combined with lazy jacks. At first I had rerouted the lines for setting the sheet downwards, using pulleys, and tied them up. But it quickly turned out to be rather impractical, because two more lines had to be tied to the mast, which is crowded already. So, now I have tied the lazy jacks to the mast and put a shackle at the stern end. The line connection is loose enough so as to not damage or chafe the expensive sheet. About a foot from the end of the lines and the shackles, I have tied one carabiner each, which makes it possible to set the system with only two moves: I just latch the carabiners directly into the shackles. This can be done from the cockpit, which increases safety on board.

PETER REMMERS, 26427 ESENS

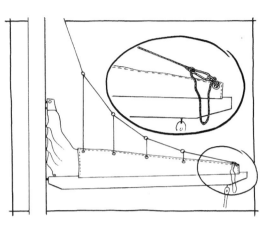

LOOSE LAZY JACKS

If you are using lazy jacks and want to have them handy at any time, you should be able to veer them enough so as to avoid noisy chafing on the seams and the sail. To avoid having to get to the mast every time, the shown solution works by simply adding a common control line below the boom head. Two rubber slings at the ends of the crosstree pull the lazy jacks far enough away when they are not in use.

FROM *YACHT* 20/00

LAZY JACKS TO TIE AWAY

Lazy jacks are quite helpful when taking down the sails before entering the port, but they also hinder the act of setting the sail on the boom and the sail cover as well as hoisting the sail—there is always some batten getting caught by the lines! The best solution is to tie them away by pulling them towards the bow under the reef hooks. In this example they are controlled in front of the mast using a central line with a guiding block.

FROM *YACHT* 20/00

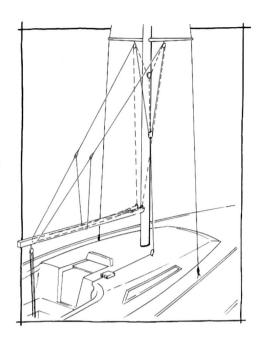

CASUALLY STOWING AWAY LAZY BAGS

As comfortable and useful as they are when setting and hauling in sails, fixed lazy jacks are rather unsightly and annoying when their respective bags are flapping empty at the boom. With a few rubber slings and a couple of minutes of work, however, they are easily stowed away.

First I veer the lines, so that they are hanging down, up to the mainsheet tack. Then I firmly roll up the covers, lines sticking out at the front end. Now I tie the sheet covers with slings to the boom—and no more unnerving lazy jacks.

DIETER BONDZUS, 24159 KIEL

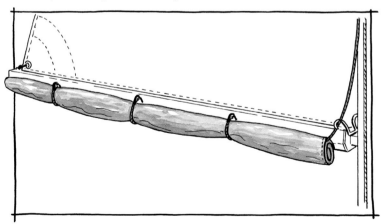

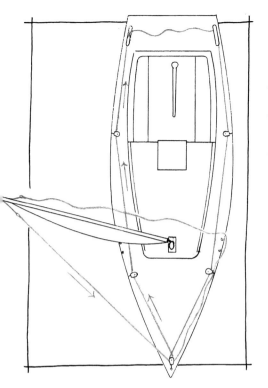

ENDLESS GYBE PREVENTER

Sailing with tailwinds is nice, but if the wind blows directly from the stern, the main boom can be rather dangerous. In this situation a gybe preventer should be set. We use an endless system which can be managed from the cockpit. We have added a double guiding block at the bow. A long line from the boom head is set past the double guiding blocks to the stern cleats. From the stern the line continues on the other side towards the bow and the double blocks around the shroud, back to the boom head. Whenever you need the gybe, you only have to haul in the corresponding side (leeward side) and put it on the cleat. While you are sailing high in the wind you can either shackle or unshackle the gybe preventer from the cockpit.

JENS KRIENKE, 22547 HAMBURG

DOUBLE GYBE PREVENTER

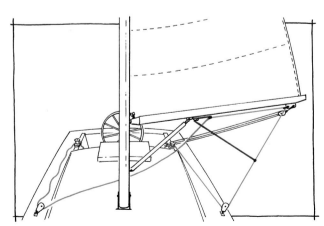

the boom head to the bow—the classic gybe preventer. This is often neglected when sailing with downwinds, where you regularly change the position of the boom. We use a double version of this safety line, one fastened to the boom head and re-routed, using guiding blocks, from the bow to the stern. In order to prevent the loose line from getting caught at the cockpit, sprayhood, or cleats on deck we have fitted a long rubber sling as a tensioner. It is latched to the gybe preventer where appropriate and re-routed via a small guiding block at the boom.

When you have an accidental gybe, the uncontrollable main boom can cause lethal injuries. To avoid this you need a safety line from

JUERGEN BOROF, 24109 KIEL

GYBE PREVENTER

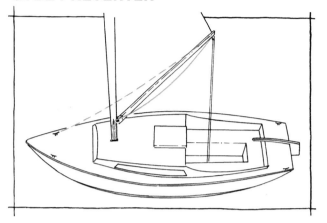

A skipper usually appreciates the comfort and safety of a gybe preventer for downwind courses

once the mainsheet has been veered out completely—and the boom head is totally out of reach. When it is latched to the boom at the front, the angle is inappropriate and the force during an accidental gybe is too great.

Lucky for you if you have a line tied to the boom head handy. This way you can easily unlatch the gybe preventer at the boom and latch it to the bow cleat. Another positive aspect: while motoring or sailing high in the wind you can use the line along the boom to latch your lifeline's carabiner.

HORST TESCHKE, 27572 BREMERHAVEN

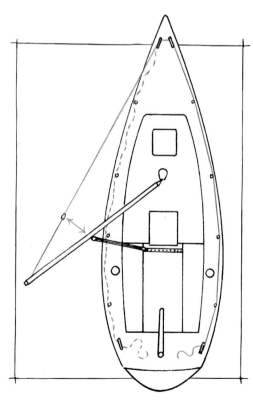

COMFORTABLE STOPPER

To prevent accidental gybes, we always set a gybe preventer. A sling at the boom makes it easy to set one up for boats with a sheet that is close to the bow. Before setting sail we place a line from a stern cleat that runs outside of the railing supports past the bow cleats, and from there back to the opposite stern cleat. Pick up the slack and hang it onto the railing. The bow cleats are used as re-routing points, so the line is not fastened. When using the gybe preventer, latch the leeward line to the boom.

To do this, use a permanently fixed sling with a carabiner latched to the boom head. The sling can be easily reached from the boat even if the mainsheet is veered out. Now you only need to haul in the slack windward line and latch the gybe to the stern cleat.

ROLF JESKE, BY EMAIL

SAFETY WITH THE GYBE PREVENTER

If you sail with stern winds and don't use the gybe preventer for safety, you are literally risking your head and neck. The easier the use of this equipment the more you are likely to take advantage of it. The pictured method requires some additional line and takes a little more time to set up. However, this gybe preventer can be quickly latched onto the boom head when switching sides.

FRIEDRICH BRUCKNER, 84453 MUEHLDORF

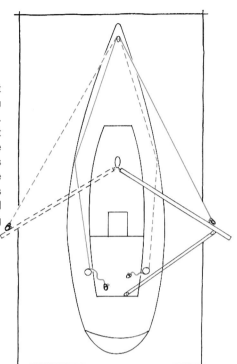

HANDLING THREE REEFING POINTS WITH ONE LINE

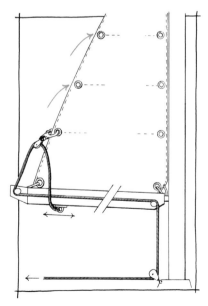

When setting and hauling in the mainsheet with permanently reeved lines, I was always bothered by the loose ends whipping around. Once the mainsheet was hauled in, I also had to stow away these lines between the folds of the sail. When setting the sail, I had to make sure that they would not hamper the process, and would clear them all the time. I solved this problem by using only one reeving line for my boat. Usually it runs loosely from the cockpit to the mast step, past the boom and to the yardarm, and from there through a shackle with a swivel fork and block to a free, self-regulating, sliding eyelet at the lower boom rail, where the line is tied with a bowline. When not in use, the shackle is latched to the jib thimble. To reef the sail, the corresponding line stopper is released, then the shackle, placing it into the appropriate reef thimble. A quick step to the mast to latch the reef thimble into the hook at the luff, and you are ready to haul in reef line and halyard. Although this system does not eliminate the trip to the mast, it certainly does away with flying lines.

EDGAR WALLENBORN, 50171 KERPEN

Editor's note: Keep in mind that this solution requires the sailor to work on a moving mainsheet at sea and might constitute an unnecessary risk.

THIRD REEF IN THE MAINSAIL WITH ONE LINE

There were many instances where we would have wanted a third reef for our HR 31, because the second one provided too much surface after force 7 Beauforts. It was not too difficult to sew a third reef into our sail, but running the reef line was not so easy. As the boom can run only two one-line systems, it would have required an outer line. The solution: because we always haul in the second reef when entering port, we could also use the slightly modified line of the first reef for the third. We mounted a hook for the bow clew at the gooseneck.

KNUD NOERENBERG, 38108 BRAUNSCHWEIG

CLAMP INSTEAD OF CLEAT

When you are reefing, things can get ugly pretty quickly, and not just on smaller boats—you tend to avoid getting to the mast. For this reason we have changed our reefing system. It used to be a classic rope for the leech as well as two hooks on the gooseneck for the reef clews at the luff of the mainsail. Now we have added more lines past the reef clews. They are tied to the reef hook on the other side while they run through a double guiding block at the mast step on this side, and from there towards the stern. Now we can control both reef points of the sail without leaving the protection of the cockpit. We could have tied them up with two cleats on the cabin deck next to the ladderway, but we wanted to save money and also avoid crowding the deck with more lines. So, we only mounted one cleat and reduced the lines with a simple trick: we combined both lines for the first and second reef after the pulleys on the cabin roof via a long-splice and put a loop onto both of them— also via a long-splice—which can just barely be placed onto the cleat after veering the luff. Then the mainsail is set. A short rubber sling attached to the cleat keeps the combination reefline handy.

VINZENZ SCHIMPFLE, 72285 PFALZGRAFENWEILE

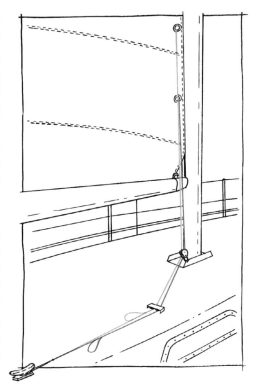

EASY REEFING

Our 32-foot yacht is fitted with a standard reef. Over time we have added a few improvements, for example, we have begun hooking the luff with a belt. Our new system saves us from having to get to the mast as well as the bothersome latching into the reef hook. Simply place an auxiliary line through the reef thimble and fasten it at the gooseneck on one side. On the other side we have mounted a guiding block with the line running through it towards the mast step. From there it is run to the halyard locks and the winches at the cockpit. In order to reef the mainsail, simply veer the halyard while at the same time hauling in the auxiliary line at the luff all the way. Then simply haul in the stern reef line. It is no problem to retrofit this two-line reef, and it is almost as comfortable to operate as a one-line system. At any rate, the mainsail can be quickly shortened during any kind of conditions directly from the cockpit. If you happen to have rings instead of the reef thimble, you can also fasten the auxiliary lines rather than threading them through the mainsail. In this case, however,

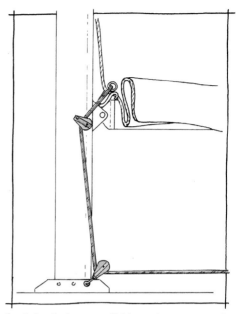

the 1:2 ratio is not available and more strength is required to tighten it.

WERNER STAHL, 70563 STUTTGART

REEFING WITHOUT CREASING

Chartered yachts are usually fitted with a furling genoa which can be quite bulky due to the additional UV protection at the foot of the sail and the leech. As there are no doublings available along the luff, the sail is rolled up pretty tightly at the top and bottom, but much less so at its center. This causes it to form a veritable "bag." Such a headsail does not allow for sailing hard into the wind and it causes considerable listing. Our solution: the forestay of the furling genoa usually features two grooves.

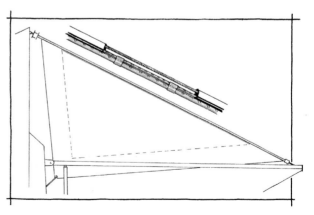

We use the available free groove to attach a half-inch "doubling line" to the thin auxiliary line to raise it at the forestay. The thin auxiliary line is fastened to the sail head and should be a little longer than the forestay. As shown in the drawing, the doubling line is tied about a foot away from the auxiliary line so that it sits outside at the forestay. Adjust the length of the doubling line so that it does not interfere in the area of the doubled luff.

WOLFGANG GOMMEL, 93057 REGENSBURG

PROTECTED REEF HOOK

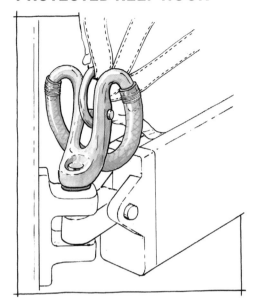

There is little argument: if you want to reef the classic way, you definitely need a double hook at the gooseneck. On our Elan 40, however, the hook is not necessary, as we use a one-line reef, but whenever we do, the luff gets caught by the hook and the sail is in danger of ripping. In order to avoid this—unfortunately, the hook cannot be removed—I have added a piece of strong plastic hose. Placed onto both ends of the hook, it forms a bow from one side to the other, preventing the sail from becoming stuck. I affixed the hose with strong nylon yarn.

MARTIN SCHUEPBACH, 2514 LIGERZ/ SWITZERLAND

LESS FRICTION

The less friction created during a maneuver the less strength you need to perform the maneuver. If you apply this rule to a boat, you will benefit from it. We even apply this when guiding our reef lines by adding small slippage pieces to the reefing clew of our mainsail and its lines. We drilled small holes below the clews, which we enlarged using a hot nail, which also sealed the holes. Then we cut strips of Teflon material to size, which we ran through the clews and affixed with screws, nuts, and washers, so that the line runs right over them.

JOHANN KLEINRATH, 2823 PITTEN/AUSTRIA

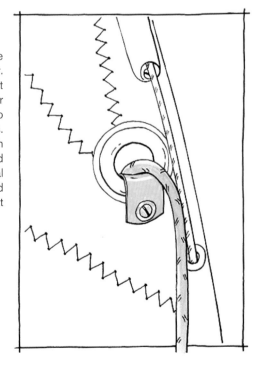

SHORT DISTANCE

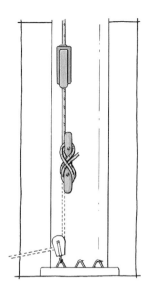

On my Hurley 800, the halyard for the furling genoa was always re-routed to the cockpit and belayed to one of the halyard stoppers. However, the halyard is actually used only at the beginning and at the end of the season, when the genoa is set or lowered. When I needed an additional reef line and space at the cleat, I simply took off the genoa to be able to tie the new line at the mast. So, I mounted a pulley below the cleat with an additional clamp for safety.

EDGAR WALLENBORN, 50171 KERPEN

Editor's note: This solution is comfortable and practical. However, the sail is stressed due to the halyard's tension and ages more quickly.

HALYARD IN THE CAMCLEAT®

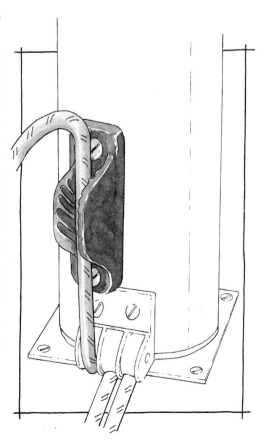

Whenever the mainsail is run with a line in the mast track, you need someone else to set the main halyard. We simply run the re-routed line to the stern and belay it to a Camcleat®, making it possible to sail single-handed. The mast stands on deck and the halyards are located at the mast step, where they run over rollers. In order to be able to run the halyard from the bow side we screwed a Camcleat® above the rollers to the mast. It can be used to belay the halyard, which is tightened manually. Back in the cockpit I pick up the slack and tighten the last few inches with the winch. Even if the mainsail is run with sliders and usually set from the stern, the cleat helps when performing this maneuver. If the weather is calm, you can work at the mast. Since the halyards are running through fewer pulleys and rollers, there is less friction, and setting the sail is easier. If the halyards exit the mast further up, then the cleat would be placed somewhat off the pulling direction between the halyard exit and the redirection.

DIETER BEHRENS, 30655 HANNOVER

PULLEY INSTEAD OF WINCH

Our small cruiser does not have halyard winches. Rather than adding an expensive after-market item, we decided to use a mobile pulley. We added a cam cleat to the upper block. To haul tight we latch the pulley to the mast step and place the halyard into the cam cleat. Now it can be hauled in without any trouble.

DIETER BEHRENS, 30655 HANNOVER

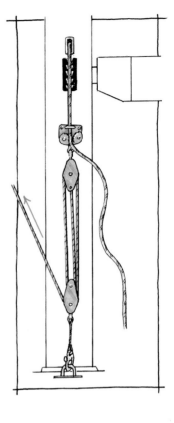

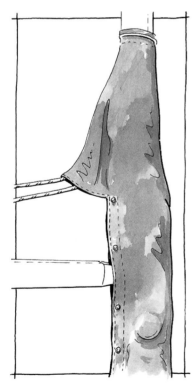

FURLING MAINSAIL TARPAULIN

When you have a furling mainsail, the clew of the rolled-up sail stays unprotected next to the mast. We sail the Mediterranean, so we don't take our boat out in winter, and we get annoyed by the dirty triangle. We leave the mainsail rolled up on the mast so the rolling axle does not bang against it when there are choppy waters.

So, we protect this section with a tarpaulin that we tie to the mast above the clew with a sturdy rubber line. The tarpaulin almost reaches the mast step and also protects the coiled-up halyards from the constant UV rays. We have added a zipper to the upper section while the lower parts towards the boom and below can be closed with Velcro® straps and push buttons.

ARRIEN TIEMON, 88677 MARKDORF

VELCRO STRAPS

The foot of our battened mainsail is about 16 feet long. To prevent it from sliding off the boom before setting it, we used to gradually unclip its net. This was rather cumbersome and involved a lot of coming and going. We solved this issue by adding two strips of Velcro® at the ends. They provide enough grip so the sail stays on the boom and they also open by themselves when setting the sail.

PETER HAECKY, 4106 THERWIL/ SCHWEIZ

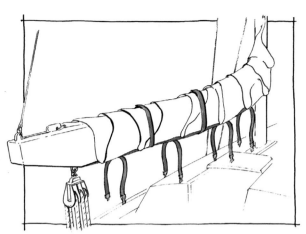

TIES WITH REMOTE CONTROL

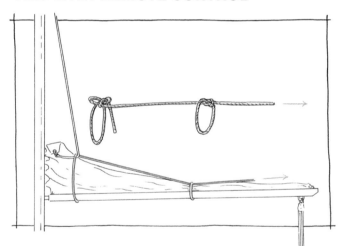

I just started sailing single-handed, so there is still plenty of room for improvement. Even though I can set the sails by myself now, I don't like to move around the deck when leaving the busy port. For the mainsail to be properly prepared on the boom, I have replaced the regular ties with a long line. I tie it around the sail, the boom, and the shackled mainsail at the bow end using a Carrick bend put to slip. Then I guide the line towards the stern and tie the sail once more with a simple Carrick bend. Once the line is ready, I start raising the mainsail slightly so the front loop stays tensioned. This prevents the halyard from getting caught by the cross tree during a swell.

When the sail is ready to be set, I first untie the stern knot, and then, with a strong pull at the line, the front slip Carrick as well. The mainsail is now ready to be set without having to leave the cockpit.

DR. FRITZ KELLER, 22417 HAMBURG

ROLLING UP THE HALYARD

The main halyard has to be either coiled up or unlatched once the sail is set, but this can be a bit of a nuisance.

The quarter-inch thick halyard now disappears through a perforation next to the mast and runs laterally in the cabin via a roll, where it disappears with the use of an old belt retractor (for old roller shutter systems, about 45 feet). I have glued the retractor below the deck, and it works great. The system has another advantage: the sail is hauled in with a slight pull and is easier to flake. This works for all types of yawl (Conger, Zugvogel, or Korsar). The line of some 20-25 feet fits nicely on the belt retractor.

GÜNTHER NOLDE, 56070 KOBLENZ

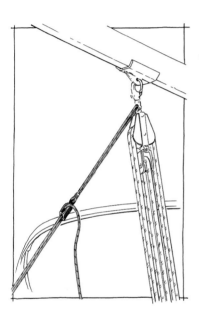

CALM MAIN BOOM

Even a slight swell causes the main boom, with its flaked sail, to go back and forth. This results in the permanent degradation of the moving parts, including chafing of the sail. Sometimes even a very tight mainsail does not help much. We limit this movement by adding an additional sling with a Camcleat®, which helps a lot with the maneuver. We push the traveller to one side and tighten the sling to the other. The resulting triangle prevents any movement.

DIETER BONDZUS, 24159 KIEL

ONE MOVE TO QUIET THE BOAT

The noise of rattling halyards is annoying for you and your neighbors at night, and the continuous chafing wears out the lines. In the case of cable halyards, the mast is also affected. To not have to deal with the topping lift and the spi halyard, we have shackled them to a loop. When we are at port, we just put it over a cleat. Tighten the halyards and things quiet down.

STEFFI VON WOLF, BY EMAIL

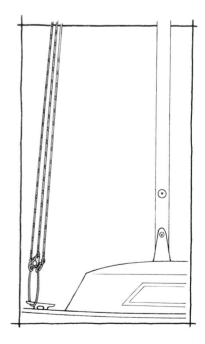

QUIET MAST CABLE

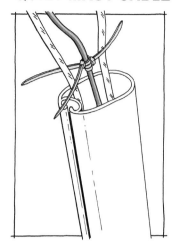

Everyone knows the evening music at port when some halyards are clanging against some mast. I used to be one of those causing this kind of noise with my Etap 20, and I received stern looks in the morning. I had tied down all the halyards and it took me a while to find the cause—the electric cable for the three-color light. I found a very simple solution to stop the noise: I tied three cable ties every two feet of the cable, with about 120 degrees between the ties. The length of the ties is about the maximum diameter of the mast. They prevent the cable from banging against the mast while not interfering with the halyards.

JAN OHLENBUSCH, 26215 WIEFELSTEDE

SIMPLE AND TIMELY CHANGE OF HALYARD

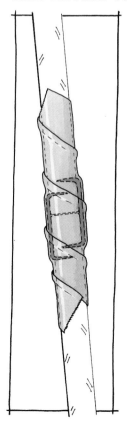

Usually a halyard tends to break at the worst possible moment. However, it tends to announce itself ahead of time, and therefore, by checking the line for chafing, it is easy to avoid. But you need to identify the cause and remove it, which is only possible if you know the areas of maximum stress (e.g., the rollers at the tip of the mast). You can prevent future problems by regularly changing this stress point and shortening the halyard now and then, leaving enough slack line from the outset.

However, you may not be able to avoid changing the halyard with a standing mast. If you do this at the right time, you save yourself the annoying threading of a pilot line from the tip of the mast. You simply tie the new halyard to the one you need to replace and carefully pull it through the mast. Sailors who don't mind elaborate halyard work use a short sling with a loop or even sew the halyards together. We have found a more simple solution: we remove the edge of the lines with a lighter, clip them together with two staples, and wrap the seam with a lot of tape. This connection is strong enough and easy to remove.

RUDOLF NAHM, 76744 WOERTH

QUICK CONNECTION TO REPLACE THE HALYARDS

There have been many suggestions about how to connect two lines with the aim of replacing halyards and auxiliary lines. The advantage of our solution is that it can be done without tools and it resists quite a bit of pulling force (e.g., when the line gets stuck while pulling it through the mast). We set the old one onto the new line and tie the lines with safety pins. Then we put tape around the area, but a few layers are enough; the connection may become too stiff otherwise.

ADELBERT NIEMEYER, 50933 COLOGNE

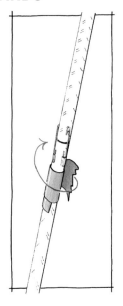

PIPE CLAMP INSTEAD OF SHACKLE

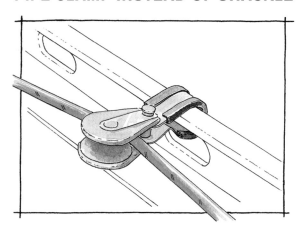

In order to bring the reef line of the furling genoa or the spi boom downhaul into the cockpit, several re-routings are often necessary. We use small guiding blocks affixed to the toe rail. In order for the anodized aluminum not to get scratched, we don't use regular shackles but small pipe clamps made from stainless steel. They are fitted with a sturdy plastic cover. To attach them to the toe rail you need to open them up a little by bending. Now you can attach the block to the clamp using a conventional bolt.

JUDITH WUNDT, BY EMAIL

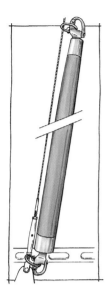

SURF MAST AS SPI BOOM

Instead of the rather unwieldy aluminum spi boom, I use a shortened fiberglass mast on my 32-foot yacht for light wind and when sailing downwind legs. The lightweight piece poses no problems and can be handled by one person. I made the fittings from stainless steel. Two turning snap shackles were welded to the end pieces, to be latched to the sail's clew and the spinnaker fitting. Unlike other places for storing it (e.g., on deck or in front of the mast), I hang it from the shroud with two stainless-steel rings. They are put on the shroud when setting the mast. I latch one end of the spi boom to the upper ring and push it up the shroud, then the lower shackle is latched to the lower ring.

DIETER BONDZUS, 24159

RING PINS

You can easily minimize the annoyance that comes with rigging up and rigging down with round, continuously bent ring pins. You can avoid the bothersome process of straightening pins out either by replacing them with the same—or better, with round ones. They can be inserted without tools and they secure the shroud tensioners just as well, provided you put them around the outside of the tensioner housing. They are also easier to manipulate.

DETLEF MEIER, 25474 BOENNINGSTEDT

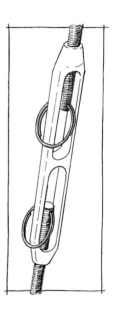

SCREWS INSTEAD OF PINS

To secure shroud tensioners so they don't become detached when twisting, simple pins are often used—but they stick out from the tensioner and need to be taped over. You should replace them every time they bend. Another possibility is safety rings, which also have to be taped over so nothing can become entangled. However, we have secured our shroud tensioners with brass screws. You have to cut a thread into the holes you drill (about 3/16 inch) and screw in two small brass bolts. The bolt heads prevent the tensioners from turning.

BRUNO EGBERT, 48432 RHEINE

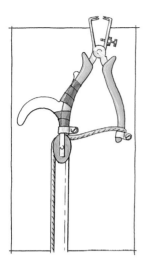

LINE CATCHER

A line can get caught high up, whether a halyard, lazy jack, or other line. You can just barely reach it with the boathook. If you have a self-opening pair of pliers, such as those used to skin electric cables, you can quickly affix it to the boathook and add a thin line to it. This allows for the pliers to be closed with the line. Use a small block for the required redirectioning.

DIETWALD SCHULZ, 70794

CLEVER KNOT

The rolling hitch is not exactly an easy knot. However, when you are in a complicated situation, such as when a line runs off your winch, you have to get it done right the first try. Another simple and effective solution comes from mountain climbing: the Prusik knot can be tied in seconds around a halyard, it locks in both directions, and it's easy to remove.

GÜNTER SINGER, 87629 HOPFEN AM SEE

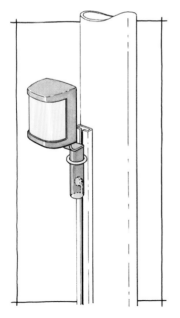

MOBILE MAST LAMP

In order to protect our mast lamp at the front side of the mast from possible damage while working on the front deck, we got a mobile variation. Our homemade adapter fits exactly into the spi boom eyelet, which we place into the topmost position on the rail, reserved for the lamp. This safeguards the light and makes it easier to service. If you need to change a lightbulb, you can do it from the comfort of your cabin.

UWE ANDRESEN, 24944 FLENSBURG

VERTICAL MAST POSITION

Usually, before trimming the mast, skippers use the mainsheet or the boom lift to measure the distance to the edge of the deck. We use a simple spring scale from the building supply retailer that we place between the halyard and the chain plate and pre-tension to about half the measuring scale. When both sides show the same value, then the "palm tree" is standing upright.

HORST ARNDORFER, 1020 VIENNA/ AUSTRIA

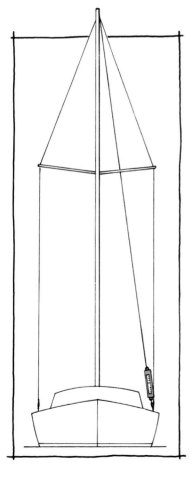

TRUNK FOR THE ETAP

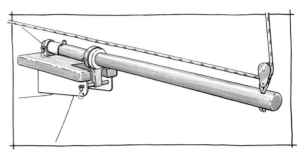

To use the gennaker of our Etap 23® more effectively, we installed a small, mobile, wooden bowsprit. It brings the sail tack further to the bow and increases the effective wind angle for our 230-sq.-ft. light sail quite noticeably (compared to the original setting, where the line was latched to the anchor winch). We had already mounted the baseplate as a step on our anchor gear to facilitate getting on board. Now it serves as the base for the stern support of our bowsprit, which terminates in a nylon sheath and can be locked with a bolt at the anchor fitting. The sprit itself consists of a 2.5-foot long and 1 3/4-inch thick round pole that can be removed from the bow plate very quickly. The pulley for the trimline of the gennaker tack is fastened with a short line to the bow perforation of the pole. We have sailed scale 4 Beaufort winds with this bowsprit without any problem. If you want to sail your gennaker with more wind, you might want to consider a larger-sized construction.

GÜNTHER WALKER, 73066 HOLZHAUSEN

NICELY WRAPPED

While transporting a boat on a trailer the rig should be tightened really well so as to not cause any chafing problems. A simple solution is to use cling wrap. It also prevents soiling of the rig. However, when storing the boat for the winter, you should not use it due to the formation of condensation.

GREGOR KAISER, 63179 OBERTSHAUSEN

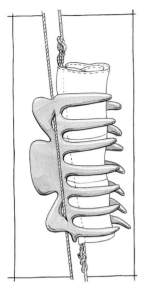

SETTING THE FOREIGN FLAG QUICKLY

If you sail close to international borders, like we do, you know that the foreign country's flag needs to be ready for use all the time. In order to affix it while not in use, we have placed a large hairclip onto the flag line. The rolled-up flag can be pinned to the line very easily. If you don't like this solution, you can use a plastic tube fitted to the size of the flag, but it is more complicated to affix it to the line or the mast.

UWE ANDERSEN, 24944 FLENSBURG

SAFELY UP THE MAST

Whether you use steps to climb into the mast, or if you are raised in a bosun's chair, you should always use a safety halyard. If you don't want to depend on a second person, you can climb up the locked halyard using a fairly expensive mountain climber's rope clamp or you can use the so-called Prusik knot. This is a knot with which you run the loop twice around the safety halyard and then through itself. When not under tension, it can be moved in both directions, and under tension it locks just like a stop knot.

CARSTEN NELL, 89231 NEU-ULM

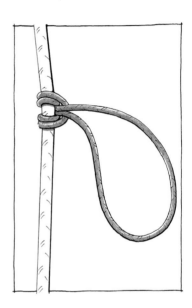

CROSSTREE LIGHTS

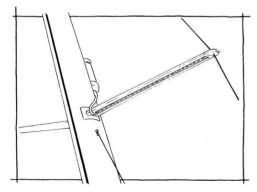

While the common lights on board illuminate the bow section of the deck, the gunwale remains in the dark. Our idea: we placed two three-foot-long, self-adhesive LED light strips on the lower side of the crosstrees and connected them to the lighting cable at the mast. These waterproof LED lights cost around 40 dollars and are very effective. In our case the light reaches out about 30 feet from the boat itself.

CHRISTOPH ZIMMERMANN, 53424 REMAGEN

STOWING & SECURING

STORING THE HATCH

There are many yachts where there is no practical space to store the hatch. We just put the Plexiglas® hatch onto the sliding hatch, but the frame of the sliding hatch had to be enlarged about half an inch. You can use a thin saw or a Dremel® fitted with a router. We place a non-slip layer between the hatches so they don't get scratched—this also prevents the hatch from moving when seas are rough. These simple modifications allow for the hatch to be always at hand, and it does not have to be taken out of the storage box or from inside the cabin.

JENS HICKSTEIN, BY EMAIL

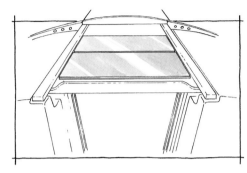

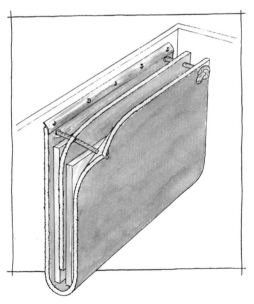

SCRATCHPROOF STORAGE

If you close your ladderway with a multi-section hatch, you know the problem: where do you put the pieces when they are not in use? With our Dehler 28 we have an additional inconvenience: the two segments consist of scratch-sensitive Plexiglas®. For some time we simply stowed both sections in the cramped storage locker, where its aspect degraded considerably. Now we have found a simple and practical solution: the vertical wall of the locker is fitted with a carpet fold that is held together by rubber slings at its top corners. We also placed another layer of carpet to separate the two Plexiglas® sections from each other. Now we can stow them away quickly and safely even if the storage locker is full to the brim.

GABRIELE KRENN, 59071 HAMM

HIDING THE HATCH

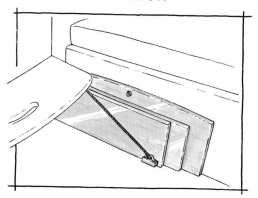

In the storage locker? On top of the dog bunk? None of these ideas are convincing, as it would be nice to keep the hatch handy and close to the ladderway—so we screwed a guiding ledge to the floor board. Now we just place the hatch sections between this ledge and the cabin wall and secure them with a rubber sling. This is a cheap and rattle-free solution that presumes that your hatch consists of several sections. Be careful with the lock: it should not rub against the wood.

HANS-GEORG CORDES, 30900 WEDEMARK

SECURING THE MAPS IN THE COCKPIT

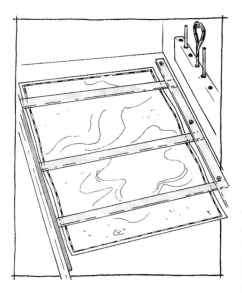

For navigation purposes we keep a small chart table in the cockpit. We once had a map blown from the boat during a moment of distraction, so I thought about building a support that would allow for working with navigation triangles and marking courses while also being easy to handle. Because of the table it was not possible to use a clear folding plate. You need several strips of Makrolon®, about an inch wide and 1/4-inch thick each, as well as a narrow, U-shaped aluminum profile the width of the chart table. Its opening is equivalent to the thickness of the Makrolon® strips. Now you mount the U-profile and one of the long strips to the front and back edges of the chart table while small washers keep the Makrolon® strips away from the table plane, so that the mobile strips can be placed under it. Cut them to match the distance between the U-profile and the facing edge. Four of them are sufficient to hold two maps on the chart table at the same time. If one of them should be in the way while marking a map, you simply shift it or pull it out and re-insert it at another place.

HELMUT WENGLER, 14129 BERLIN

HIDDEN MAP COMPARTMENT

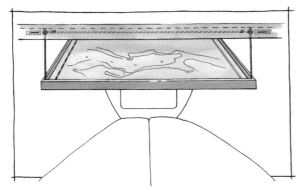

Stowing away ocean maps and charts is always an issue on any boat, but more so on small ones. I found a solution for our Dehler 28 that saves space and puts them out of the way while allowing quick access. I used mahogany profiles and a white fiber board to build a frame with a size that fits exactly below the bow cabin roof. I used three hinges to affix this picture frame–like box below the cabinet so it can be opened and lowered. There are two latches that lock the flap when it is closed. Two thin lines at the frame and the ceiling prevent it from opening all the way. If the lines bother you, add a rubber band so they are pulled inwards when the frame is closed. Make sure that the size of your chart frame allows for other storage doors and drawers to be opened without a problem.

GABRIELE KRENIN, 59071 HAMM

VERTICAL DOCUMENT COMPARTMENT

Often the marine charts are not the only items stored in the flat compartment of the chart table, but other navigation documents as well. In this case, the search for the corresponding charts turns into an exercise of rummaging around. If you have space for a translucent vertical chart compartment at the bulkhead, you can make things easier. It consists of a large pane and three strips of Makrolon. You can affix it quickly with a couple of screws and it requires very little space.

HELMUT WENGLER, 14129 BERLIN

OVERHEAD STORAGE OF MAPS AND CHARTS

In many instances, ocean maps are kept together with other navigational documents in the narrow map compartment. Whenever you have to search for a particular map, you start rummaging through the pile. It is rare to have additional storage space for thicker stacks of maps, and rolling them up individually takes up even more space. This can be solved with a compartment under the ceiling of the cockpit or over

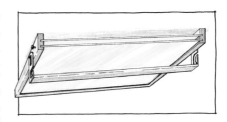

the bunks in the bow cabin. If you add another layer to the frame, it is a lot easier to sort them. When you build the lid, make sure you have a secure closing mechanism.

HEINZ HAMANN, 21709 DUEDENBUETTEL

WELL-SECURED

To use the space on our yacht efficiently, we keep beverage containers in the bilge. The area under the floor boards is also the coolest on the boat. However, when these bottles are packed loosely, they tend to roll around. We avoid this by adding compartments made from foam rubber. Place one strip of foam into the bilge, and several compartments are added by implementing vertical strips of the same material. Use a strong glue to affix the contact surfaces. Surrounded on three sides by foam, these bottles are cushioned well now. They can't roll around the bilge anymore; broken bottles are a thing of the past.

HERMANN BOEHM, 53797 LOHMAR

CONTAINER FOR PARTS IN THE LOCKER

My suggestion will provide you with a solution to keep things in order and handy. I keep the winch handles in the storage locker whenever we are not sailing. I made a small compartment from wood and placed it close to the upper edge so as not to have to bend down so much. Now the handles and other items are comfortably stowed away and always within reach.

HARTMUT POHL, 22397 HAMBURG

Editor's note: This also works without having to build anything. You can simply mount some robust fabric bags, which can be found at many retail stores, to the area described by Hartmut Pohl.

BULKHEAD STORAGE

Over time the crew's predilections change, which is directly related to the kind of beverages you take with you. A summer family trip requires different bottles than for a men-only outing. For this reason we have fitted our beverage bunk with various compartments. Depending on how many compartments you prefer, cut several plywood boards to the shape of the bulkhead. Drill through the boards at the edges and thread them onto three long-threaded rods. Nuts and washers on both sides of the bulkhead provide the required stability. In order to install the compartments, place them all together. This results in a flexible construction that can be manipulated with the open bulkhead cover. Then place the compartments at the desired distance and tighten the nuts.

FRED SOMMER, 22523 HAMBURG

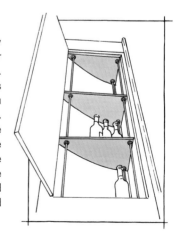

WOODEN FRAME FOR LAPTOP

If you like wood, you might prefer a laptop frame in which you may cut out the required sections for cable connections in the sides and/or rear section yourself. Two small rubber rollers keep the screen open. The trick with this mounting is the lateral metal angles that are mounted to the bottom of the chart table; this way the entire frame can be shifted to the back or taken off the table.

WOLFGANG PRUEMMER, 52351 DUEREN

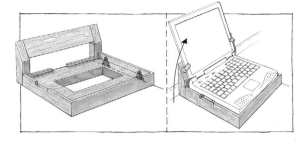

GREAT LAPTOP GRIP

Affix the computer with Velcro® onto a wooden plate that has a no-slip fabric glued to its bottom. Under normal circumstances the laptop stays safely on the chart table. If conditions are really rough, you should add a round nub that fits into the hole of the chart table.

HARALD GRAF VON SAURMA-JELTSCH, 24941 FLENSBURG

PC TURNTABLE

Using Velcro® to safely secure a laptop on the chart table is a great idea (YACHT 25/04, page 82). The disadvantage is that the computer is fixed in one position and it is hard to read the screen from an angle. For this reason we have added a turning table onto the chart table and glued the Velcro® straps to it, running them over the laptop. Such rotating baseplates for monitors can be purchased in several sizes at low cost. Now it is easy to turn the display to any angle, be it towards the ladderway for the navigator or as a monitor or DVD player for the salon. These rotating base plates tend to turn lightly with any movement, so we removed the ball bearing.

THOMAS DORN, 22395 HAMBURG

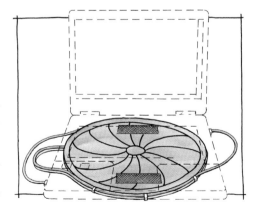

LAPTOP HOLDER

It is almost impossible to imagine the navigation routine on board without a laptop. We are among those people who want to have our computer with us during chartered trips. However, most of the presented methods are not suited to secure the practical but delicate laptop on the chart table. We have been using the following method for years, and it is cheap and does not require any storage space. We bought a self-adhesive Velcro® band and put four small strips with the rough side up at the spot on the chart table where the laptop is supposed to go, then glued the corresponding Velcro® sections to the bottom of the laptop. This ensures that it stays put even during stormy weather conditions. At the end of the trip we simply peel off the Velcro® sections from the table and put them under the laptop.

RAINER JUETTNER, 71732 TAMM

AFFIXED WITH A RUBBER SLING

Our Acer laptop has quickly become an indispensable part of navigation. So, we try to provide the best possible safety in a simple way: a sturdy rubber sling runs across the open laptop's hinge with two plastic hooks that lock into eyelets screwed into the cabin wall. To protect the rear cables and connections, we place a block of foam between the laptop and the wall with cutouts at its lower edge.

PETER REINKE, 28777 BREMEN

BOXES ON THE SHELF

In case the boat builder has left empty space between the lockers and the deck, say, about the width of a hand, it is usually poorly secured with a low ledge. There may even be some open space in the rear that can cause small items between the locker and the hull to disappear forever. You can make great use of this small space by using flat drawers for additional storage.

HANS KAMMERER, 69124 HEIDELBERG

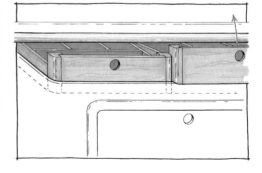

STEPPED CUPBOARD

For many boats the area in front of the ladderway is an important place around the chart table, wetroom, pantry, and salon. This is a good area to be able to put all kinds of things and have them handy. On our Dehler 28, we have added triangular lateral supports to form an additional storage space via a folding cupboard made from plywood. The lower screws function as hinges, and a latch holds it when it is closed.

GABRIELE KRENN, 59071 HAMM

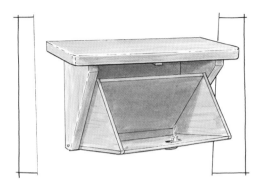

SEAWORTHY DRINKING GLASSES

Whenever things become a little agitated at sea, we don't want to have to worry about our drinking glasses. So, we built ourselves a storm-proof glass rack. We screwed six round wooden knobs to a board and covered them with felt. The rear side of the board is covered with Velcro® so it can be affixed to a cupboard. It is easy to take out, too. Now, even with stormy outings, we don't have any more broken glass and can enjoy our final toast.

PETER HAECKY, 4106 THERWIL/SWITZERLAND

BOOK SUPPORT

If your bookshelf is only halfway full, it will most likely be moving about quite a lot. Even the ledge halfway up the bookshelf will not help much. But if you cut a center groove into the ledge, you can add a round piece of wood fitted with a threaded bolt, two washers, and a knob. This allows for supporting any number of books and prevents them from falling out.

REINER WIRSCHING, 52078 AACHEN

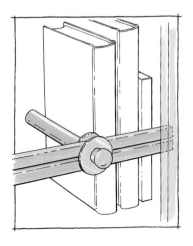

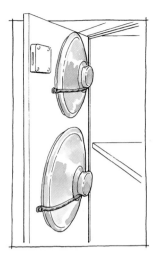

WELL-SECURED

All our cooking gear is stored in the cupboard below the sink, and it only fits if all of the pots are placed inside each other. This requires the lids to be separate from the pots, and they tend to roll around even while at port. We can always bet that the one lid we need right now has disappeared into the back of the open storage cupboard. So, we have to perform gymnastics and stretch to get it back. We came up with the following solution: we affixed rubber slings to the interior face of the cupboard doors to hold the round tops. Now we have complete "lid discipline."

ARRIEN TIEMON, 88677 MARKDORF

PRACTICAL SUPPORTS

Our boat features an open shelf above the back rests of our salon, with high ledges that make it suitable for keeping books. The shelf is never full, so the books keep falling over in groups or even fall out of the shelf. Filling the empty shelf with other items did not help much. Small plywood boxes changed that, and their depth fits that of the shelf. This prevents the books from falling out, while there is also plenty of room to store all kinds of items that would otherwise be rolling around in cupboards or drawers. Interior walls help to keep things tidy. We built the storage boxes from plywood scraps, which we glued together. A handle between the lateral sides helps to take out the boxes.

FRITZ BORMERSHEIM, 29223 CELLE

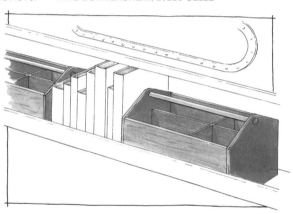

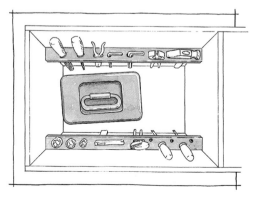

ORDER WITH LIMITED SPACE

Our boat has only a few storage lockers, and none of them has the right size for a conventional toolbox. So, we outfitted the box below the navigation seat. We screwed ledges of about 2.5 inches width to the lateral walls and added holes and openings for all of the tools by drilling and shaping. There's even room in the center to keep a container for miscellaneous items.

HERMANN BOEHM, 53797 LOHMAR

DRAWERS FOR MISCELLANEOUS ITEMS

It is almost inevitable: almost every small storage space on board quickly fills up with useful and not so useful items. Most of the time it is a collection of small pieces that tends to form a random mix. If you need any of the parts, you will have to start rummaging around. If the cupboard is the open kind, then you might even have these parts flying around your cabin when the next gale hits the boat. So, we have built a few small drawers from glued plywood sections

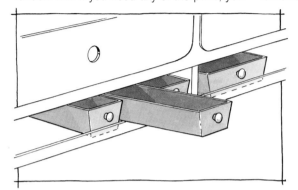

that are just about high enough to fit into the opening of the cupboard or tray. The ledges of the tray prevent the boxes from sliding out. Everything stays in place during heavy seas and the boxes help a lot to keep things grouped together and able to be found more quickly.

FRITZ BORMERSHEIM, 29223 CELLE

SAFE AND WITHIN REACH

Glasses (spectacles) are invaluable but delicate items when boating. With all the different varieties, such as reading glasses, the spare pair, sunglasses, and so on you quickly end up with quite a few valuable and fragile optical assistants. But where do you keep glasses on board so you can put them away safely and reach for them in a second? We built ourselves a central board for them, mounted in the navigation area at the hatch.

Take a thin plywood board, screw a few 1.5-inch long round pegs to it (from the back), and add two slightly tensioned rubber slings lengthwise, held in place by two ledges at the top and bottom. Now place the temples of the glasses behind both the rubber slings (one of them may be sufficient) and the nosebridge onto the round peg. You can use the gaps in between the glasses to fit in even more pairs.

SEBASTIAN KOPIEZ, 44267 DORTMUND

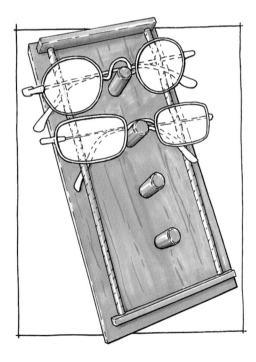

SECURED DRAWERS

A good boating drawer should actually come already prepared for not sliding out or even falling off entirely during heavy seas. But this is not always the case, and you might find out only after having the content of a drawer all over the cabin floor. You can easily fix this. There are several kinds of latches and locks available. We had to find a different solution because latches required drilling holes into the drawer and a sliding bar did not work either. We added very basic turning woodblocks that are screwed to the fascia boards of the drawer's frame. We tune the friction of these blocks by tightening the screws.

WALTER CLASEN, 22605 HAMBURG

SECURED IN CASE OF HEELING

Fixed plate racks with their centers cut out are quite practical for grabbing over the pantry, but, due to their basic construction, there is always the possibility that the topmost plates will slide out of the gap between the top edge of the pantry and the ceiling. They will likely break on your cabin floor or at least leave unsightly scratches and dents.

To close the gap above the pantry, we built a simple additional board from plywood sections that can easily be placed. The short sections inside the cutouts provide a nice positioning when putting in the closing plate. The outer ledge is simply held via two wingnuts. In case we need a couple of plates we simply loosen the outer ledge, slide the board downward, and then put it back up to secure the pantry.

PETER HAECKY. 4106 THERWIL/SCHWEIZ

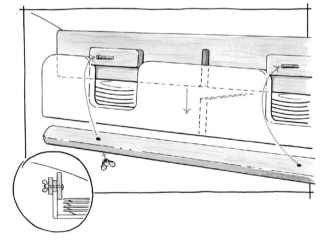

KEEP IT BOXED!

Our Bavaria 36 doesn't really have any good storage space for books and nautical literature. The existing cupboards are used for other purposes, and the height of the other ones is not sufficient to add a fiddle to them. So, I built a bookcase below the cupboards and set it into the rack just above the back upholstery of the salon bunk. The box is made from plywood sections that are glued together using thick epoxy resin. A ledge around the box prevents it from falling through the cutout. We stained and varnished all of the visible surfaces of the box, which is roomy enough for quite a few books, including office-size folders.

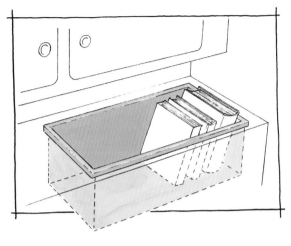

CLAUS-ULRICH FLEBBE, 69151 NECKARGEMUEND

ORGANIZED PAPERWORK

Every season we sail the North and Baltic seas for several weeks. This is a great time to catch up on reading the many magazines that pile up over time, so we always bring along quite a few of them. Add to that the daily additions of regional newspapers, and you get quite a pile. Until now we had this issue concerning where to put all this paper. Our cupboards are all full, and we didn't want to rummage through them every time we wanted something.

We came up with the idea to build a magazine stand. There was a good space for it under the salon table. A carpenter built us a shelf that fit exactly between the lowered table plates and was affixed to the round table leg with a plastic clip—but you can certainly build such a shelf rack yourself. The bottom side is covered with felt so it does not get scratched. The entire magazine rack can be removed with just one maneuver, so the regular bilge check is not a problem. Since we got this onboard news kiosk, there are now far fewer editions that remain unread, and one or the other port manual now has its standard space in our centrally located magazine rack. This works a lot better and quicker than having these items inside a cupboard at the navigation table.

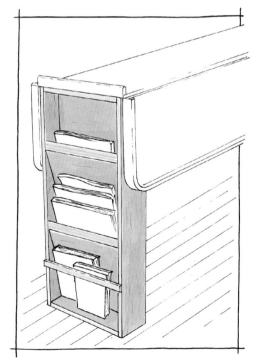

DORIS TWARDZIOK, 25938 WYK AUF FOEHR

SEAWORTHY SHELF

Bookshelves are often secured with wooden ledges, but in order to get to one book, you have to remove the entire ledge. A securing line is much more practical; it is fixated using a small plastic stopper, as used with nautical clothing. Just loosen the line a little to take out a book.
DIETER BEHRENS, 30655 HANNOVER

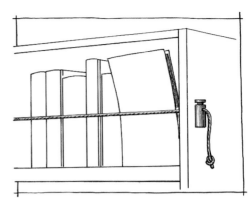

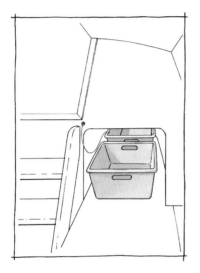

BOX CONNECTION

We use the dog bunk on our small cruiser as a readily accessible storage space for oilskins, spare clothing, rubber boots, and other items we keep in plastic boxes. As the dog bunk is rather narrow, getting to the rear box is always annoying. We added a short line to the rear box, and now there is no more uncomfortable fishing around the dog bunk.
JOHANN KLEINRATH, 2823 PITTEN/AUSTRIA

ORDER IN THE WARDROBE

Many boats feature wardrobes that are simply too small, so you tend to stuff the clothing together in order to fit it in. The result is that sleeves and other parts of jackets and coats stick out and get entangled when you close the door. We have solved this by adding a simple ledge, which we have attached with two small wooden blocks on the left and right of the lateral walls at about the center of the wardrobe's total height. They keep the clothing that sticks out in check while providing support during choppy seas.
GÜNTER HAMANN, 21709 DUEDENBUETTEL

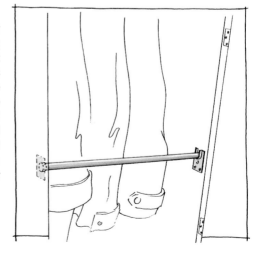

MOBILE LADDERWAY

Most yachts have little spare space available. It is known that the smaller the boat, the more organized the storage space needs to be. The space below the cockpit is huge on our Etap 23i, but until now we could hardly use it, because the fixed steps of the ladderway make it difficult to reach. This resulted in quite a mess. Also, the cooler that was placed there could not be fully opened. In order to improve the access we mounted the lowest step of the ladderway onto a roller board that can be pulled out like a drawer. We also added rollers to the lateral sides

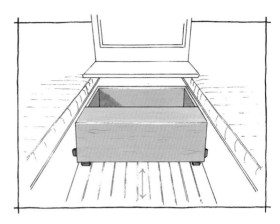

of the box, so it can be opened when there is a lot of list. Two latches, left and right, lock the step in place, so the drawer does not open even during heavy seas. We dramatically improved the use of space, and the cooler can be opened without any problem.

STEFAN JOCKENHOEVEL, 52072 AACHEN

VENTILATED SHOE LOCKER

Where do you put all your shoes? Particularly aboard small boats, shoes are often put wherever there is any free space. On our Dehler Delanta 80, we added three levels of wooden rods (about a 1/2-inch thick) between the ladderway's lowest step and the wall of the toilet next to it by drilling holes into the lateral wall between the step and the separating wall. We found the best positions by trying them out beforehand. The rods are glued into the holes. Now slippers and shoes have their space and don't fly around anymore. They are well-ventilated, can dry quickly if necessary, and are always within reach.

THOMAS PETRI, 65933 FRANKFURT

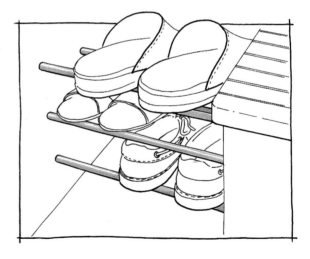

SECURED CUPBOARD

Snap locks and latches on lids and flaps are a handy feature—they open and close easily. The disadvantage is that objects inside the drawer can touch the latch and open it, which causes the content to be spilled all over the cabin floor. A small spacer around the latch can solve this problem. We added a cable pipe section cut in half and affixed it with putty.

JUERGEN SANDKUHL, 28844 WEYHE

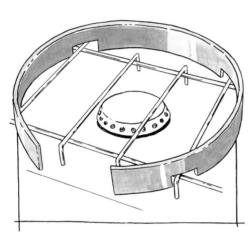

SIMPLE POT HOLDER

If you want to use your cooker while sailing, you need to secure the cooking utensils. The pot holders suitable to our stove are no longer available, so we have made some strips from soft metal. The ring lies on top of the grill with its four grooves. Before firing up the stove we adjust the diameter to the pot we are going to use. In heavy seas this is not sufficient to secure our pots, but our kitchen is closed under such circumstances anyway.

EDGAR WOHLHEBEN, BY EMAIL

SUPPORT FOR SPECTACLES/GLASSES

"Now where did I put my reading glasses/sunglasses?" To avoid the annoying search in the cabin or the cockpit, we have affixed them to the sprayhood's braces. We just hang the glasses, with one of the temples over the thin line, hooking them into the knots we put in. This way, they don't slide around with heavy seas. The line is also perfect for storing and drying sailing gloves, which are placed using Velcro® straps.

BARBARA DANNEHL, 63150
HEUSENSTAMM

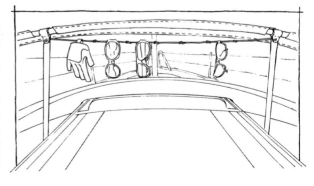

KEEPING THE ANCHOR BOX IN ORDER

Just like all storage lockers, large anchor boxes are prone to disorder; the larger they are, the more you put into them. We used the simplest methods to assure some order so we don't have to deal with such a mess and rummage around when we need an item. The center of the space is occupied by a six-inch high, pyramid-shaped box. It is made from 3/4-inch thick plywood boards and offers a secure space for the sliding weight of the anchor. It also provides space to coil up the anchor halyard around it. Our 25-pound Brittany anchor is placed upwards against the sloping hull wall and is secured with short lines and cushioned with hard foam towards the hull.

The electrical connection of our Hurley 800 is also inside the anchor box. This is not really the best place due to corrosion, but the boat came that way from the shipyard. We coiled up the cable and tied it to two aluminum hooks at the rear wall of the box, which also holds a ball fender.

EDGAR WALLENBORN,
50171 WALLENBORN,
50171 KERPEN

DINGHY WITH HANDLES

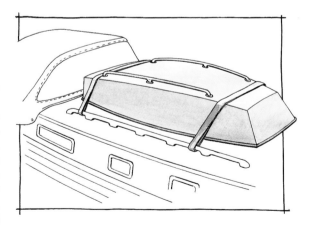

Where do you put a solid dinghy if you don't want to trail it behind? This is one of the disadvantages of a rigid dinghy: it can't be folded together to save space. If you happen to have sufficient space between the mast and the sprayhood, you are fortunate—you can turn the dinghy (an Optimist in our case) upside down and tie it down. We also mounted two additional handrails made from stainless steel below the outer edges of the dinghy to increase safety. Not only do they improve the fit of the dinghy, they also provide an additional grip at the right height for the crew during heavy seas, when they need to reach the bow. Make sure that the handrails are really well anchored for this kind of setup.

SEEN AT THE PORT OF HORUPHAV/DENMARK

COOL PARKING: STERN SUPPORT FOR BICYCLES

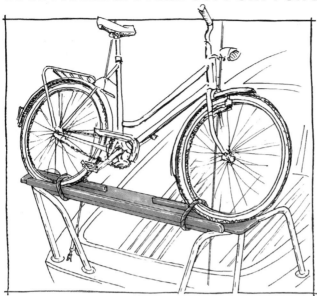

Small boats do not offer a lot of storage space. The storage lockers are already filled with the anchor, propane tank, and the outboarder gasoline tank. The sails are kept on the foreship and the duffel bags under the bunks. So, how about two bicycles for land tours? Usually there is no space for them. If you keep them next to the bow railing, they are in the way of the headsail. If you place them further to the stern, they bother the crew when sitting on the cockpit coaming. There might be some space in the cabin, but who wants to invest in space-saving collapsible bikes for a two-week vacation? Better not to have any bikes at all. However, if any mid-sized car is able to transport bicycles for a family of four, then a small cruiser should offer some sort of solution as well.

Today, bikes are frequently transported by affixing them to the back of a car. This should also work for boats: prepare a board with the needed drilled holes, mount it to the stern pulpit and the backstay (if there is one), and tie it down so it cannot slip. The bikes lean on the backstays and are secured with rubber slings, and ledges screwed to the board prevent the bikes from moving around. When at port, they are ready for use and stowed away again just as quickly. Boats with only one backstay need additional support lines, and Bergstroem rigs without backstays are not suited for this type of bicycle support. The position of the bikes may be rather complicated if you need to moor "Roman-Catholic" style.

Caution: Bike parts that stick out from the backstays, such as handles, saddles, and pedals, must not impede the free movement of the mainsail—you may have to turn them away or take them off. This construction has become fairly popular at port, and there have not been any safety problems so far.

KURT HOFFMANN, 33611 BIELEFELD

BOX FOR GPS OR CELLPHONE

A GPS device is very practical to have on board. We have built a mobile waterproof support for the steering column for when we charter yachts. The box and the lid are made from high-density foam sections that are easy to cut and glue together. We painted the outer surfaces and glued a window made from thin Plexiglas® foil into the lid. There are also small Velcro® straps at the top and bottom of the lid. The column consists of aluminum tubing, and the clamp was milled from solid aluminum. You can also use PE, which is easier to work with. The bolts are available at hardware stores.

DIETER SCHITTKO, 93073 NEUTRAUBLING

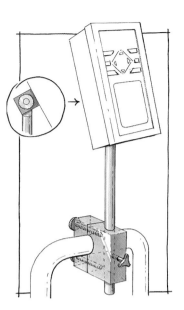

DINGHY PARKING SPACE

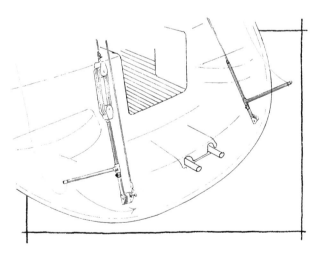

In most cases you cannot avoid bringing along a dinghy. We got tired of packing it away or lifting it onto the foreship of our Bavaria 38, and trailing it is not a good option either. I chose to modify our two-part stern backstay: the steel cables where shortened by about a foot and replaced by 1-inch stainless-steel strong tubes with welded end-pieces. Two turning supports are mounted on these tubes with a T-connector acting as the hinge. We only added a small groove to it, so it locks with a welded bolt when the support is extended. Now the dinghy can be placed from the bathing platform without any problem. Secure it with two lines.

ARMIN HORN, 73728 ESSLINGEN

PANTRY & SALON

OPTIMIZED SALON TABLE

When we bought our Shark 24 about a year ago, its interior needed some serious refurbishing. One important detail involved implementing a new table system. We quickly found out that none of the standard folding mechanisms would work for us. Either they took up too much space or the tables were simply too small. So, we had to come up with our own system.

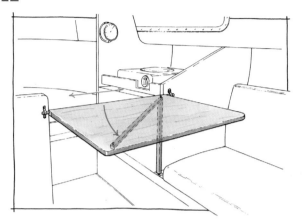

This is how it works: we created a slit for the table to fit below the gas stove's bottom plate and the drawer beneath. It fits between the dividing panels of the bunk beds or sofas, where they are fastened with two fittings. The horizontal support is provided by a swiveling stainless-steel arm with a 90-degree angle. It can be turned and fastened in two different positions and is attached to the small front pantry section. Whenever we need it, we place it under the table plate where it locks with a small nut. If we don't need it we take off the plate, unlock the fittings, and put it under the stove. The swiveling arm swings its horizontal section, so as to prevent the plate from sliding out from its place. ELFRIEDE KISCH, 2340 MOELDING/AUSTRIA

FLYING COUNTERTOP

Working space on a boat is pretty rare. We created more space in our pantry by fitting a piece of plastic to a wooden board so that it can sit on a cupboard and doesn't slip towards the center of the boat. The opposite side is tied to the cabin's ceiling handle with a line, so there is no need for an additional point of support. We painted the resulting extra countertop board in white, matching the boat, and it is ready for action in mere seconds. Whenever it is not in use, it can be easily stored away.
MICHAEL KRUSE, BY EMAIL

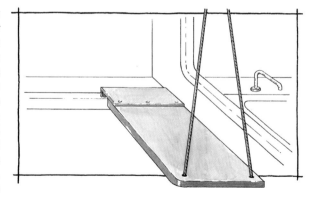

TABLE AND TRAY

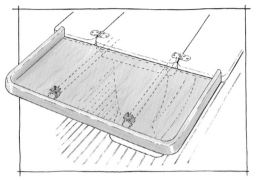
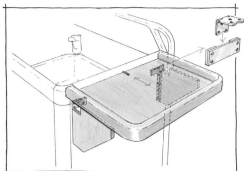

Space for working and for putting things in the pantry is usually very scarce on boats. We not only wanted to enlarge the kitchen, but also have a tray we could use to make the cockpit table somewhat bigger. So, we added a lateral board to the sink of our Bavaria 37 cruiser; it can be placed upright via hinges and two folding supports. The hinges are not permanently affixed to the sink; rather, they are placed into stainless-steel brackets. An adjustable safety pin secures the plate from slipping out of these brackets; if you remove the safety pin, you can use the plate as a tray. The bottom side of the cockpit table already had two lengthwise grooves we replaced with 3/4-inch stainless-steel tubes. When they are extended, they serve as the support for the tray, which can be easily clipped on. When they are retracted, they are perfectly out of the way.

ARMIN HORN, 71272 RENNINGEN

WORKBENCH IN THE FORESHIP

Skippers who like to do handiwork often miss having a sturdy vise on board. We have found the following solution: Cut out a solid plywood plate so that it fits exactly into the foreship's seat. Drill several holes into the plate to fasten the vise with countersunk head screws so that the seat will not become damaged. Nuts are placed on the top side to fasten the vise. In order to perform tasks, turn the plate with the vise around and tighten it with three latches. If you need the space to sit or to sleep on, simply turn the plate upside down again and cover it with the upholstery.

EDGAR WOHLHEBEN, BY EMAIL

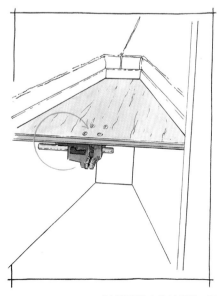

COVER PLATE AS A WORK SURFACE

Virtually all of the pantries combined don't offer enough space to work and to store things. On top of that, you will rarely find a surface that can take a few dents or a slipped screwdriver. We didn't want to sacrifice the chart table or the salon table for this application, so we found a solution by making a one-inch strong cover plate from plywood, laminated with veneer and fitted with a teak rim, to put on top of our gimbal-suspended stove. Not only is it useful as a space for loose items, but it can also be used as a mobile working surface—wherever you can fit it. If the work involved is a bit rough, we simply turn it upside down so we don't have to worry about the veneer getting damaged. We built the rim so it sticks out on both surfaces, which

prevents screws and other round parts from rolling off.

HARTMUT POHL, 22397 HAMBURG

LAPTOP ON THE MAST

On smaller yachts it is difficult to find a feasible position where a laptop can be placed safely, and which allows for daily navigation tasks. Our solution: we built a small wooden support frame that holds the laptop and prevents it from moving. The support is screwed to the mast using simple steel angles and pipe clamps. This solution does not require permanent modifications of the boat, and the display is easy to read.

BERNHARD UHRMEISTER, 30419 HANNOVER

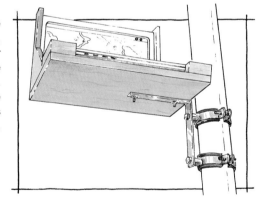

COFFEE FILTER HOLDER

On our very basic small cruiser we make coffee by brewing it in a thermos bottle right in front of the ladderway, as there are no other good places on board. However, there is always the risk of it tipping over. To prevent this, we built a holder that can be pushed under the step of the ladderway whenever it is not in use. It consists of a small plywood board with the appropriate round cutout and is screwed under the step.

WILFRIED KORFF, 40489 DUESSELDORF

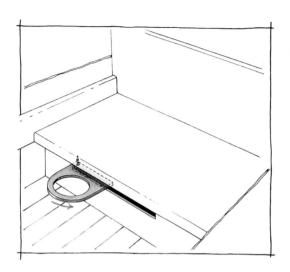

FIXED FILTER

This simple method prevents the content of the filter from spilling all over the place whenever there is even the slightest wave. We place a rubber sling around the faucet, then around the filter, and finally latch it onto a small screw at the front of the sink. To prevent the rubber from slipping off the filter, we threaded two nuts to limit the loop.

GERHARD STANDOP, 50859 COLOGNE

SECOND SINK

Because we have only one sink in our pantry, we use a plastic bucket to put the dishes in. Due to restricted space we had to place it on the floor. After getting tired of bending down, I developed a mobile support that makes it possible to place the bucket at the right height. I built a U-shaped mahogany frame with two stainless-steel rods (1/4-inch thick) in it, so it can be pushed onto the bushings set into the front wall of the pantry.

HEINZ HAMANN, 21709 DUEDENBUETTEL

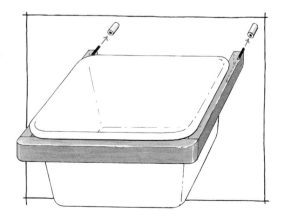

SEAWORTHY TOWEL HOLDER

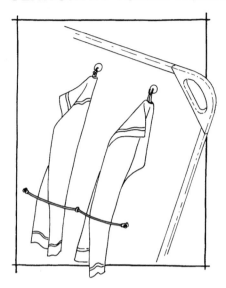

During heavy seas the towels in the pantry or the bathroom are in the way and even pose a security risk. This is why we used to take off the towels before leaving port and stored them away. Now we have found a better solution: we tension a thin rubber line across the lower third of the towel spaces, which keeps the towels in place even during heavy weather, and they are always ready for use. They also dry more quickly than when they are folded together in the cupboard.

JANINE ROSENBERGER, 10707 BERLIN

ELEGANT STOPPER

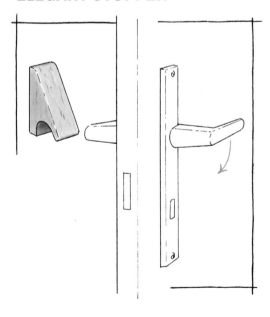

We often leave the door to the stern cabin open for better ventilation. However, it tends to move around with the slightest movement of the boat. Slamming doors are not only annoying, but also wear out the hinges rather quickly. Many boatbuilders use metal hooks to lock them, but they tend to have some play, so the doors might move a little and start to rattle with even light swells.

We solved this problem with a small wooden wedge with a V-shaped groove cut into its bottom face. The wedge can be affixed to the wall using double-sided adhesive tape. Choose the height of the wedge so it is slightly below the door handle. The spring mechanism of the handle automatically centers it in the V-shaped groove, and the door is prevented from rattling. You can make this wedge from wood that matches the interior design. It costs very little and it is also much less obvious than a chromed brass hook.

BORIS AMSTAD, 6048 HORW/SWITZERLAND

SPLATTER GUARD FOR THE STOVE

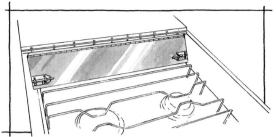

When cooking and frying food, the space behind the stove gets dirty quickly—and it is difficult to reach. To prevent this from happening we have added a metal sheet, or splatter, guard. When using it at sea, the stove would not be able to swing freely if the sheet were affixed completely. The splatter guard is attached at the top with a piano hinge, and at the bottom it either sits on the stove or it swings freely in the empty space behind the stove, and it is held in place with bolts. This position is essential when using the oven to provide the necessary air circulation.

BRIGITTE LANGE. BY EMAIL

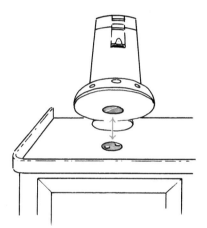

MAGNET HOLDER

We use a coffee grinder on board. To affix it so it does not move around during swells, we use magnet plates, such as those provided for smoke alarms. These plates can be purchased at building material suppliers for about seven dollars. Simply affix them with the included adhesive tape. The advantage of these magnetic plates on the countertop is that you can mount and dismount objects repeatedly.

MICHAEL BREUER, 13187 BERLIN

BOWDEN CABLE FOR THE SEACOCKS

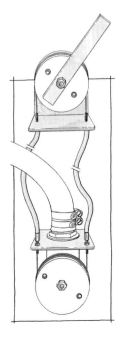

It is important to be able to close the seacocks at any time for safety reasons, but on many yachts, they are quite difficult to reach—on our boat they are practically hidden between the false floors of the aft peak—so we have come up with a remote control. We made some plastic cable sheaves to replace the lever. The counterbearings for the bowden cable sheaves are made from aluminum plates, which are drilled with holes to fit the thread of the hose connectors and are placed between the seacock and the hose. Both bowden cables and adjustment screws come from motorcycle parts. The handle also consists of a cable sheave fastened with a bolt to the aluminum plate. The flexible bowden cables allow for the seacocks to be opened and closed from easily accessible areas.

MANFRED SCHMIDT, 24107 STAMPE

DIRECT ACCESS

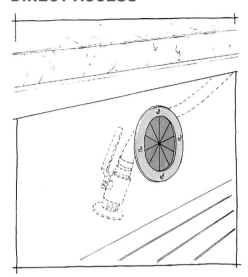

Seacocks are often placed below the bunks. Whenever they need to be handled, you need to remove the foam pads and the bunk boards. To avoid this annoying procedure, we have drilled a hole into the wall of the bunk. Now we can put our hand through the wall and reach the seacock without problems. We installed a round wooden frame with a rubber plate (with slits cut into it) so the hole looks a lot better. A wooden box prevents the seacock from being blocked by loose items.

HEINZ HAMANN, 21709 DUEDENBUETTEL

EMERGENCY SUPPLY FROM THE WATER TANK

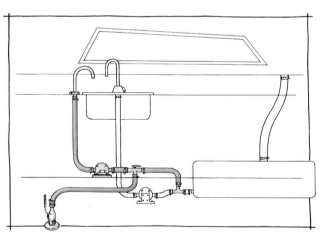

The water supply system on our 36-foot yacht features an additional pedal-operated pump whose output reaches the sink via a separate rotating faucet. This is not only suitable for saving water, but also makes it possible to provide an emergency water supply in case the electric system fails or the water pump is damaged beyond repair. This pedal-operated water hose was connected to the water system, so whenever you opened a faucet on the boat and the main water pump turned on, water dripped from the additional faucet. Not only did this increase water consumption, but in case we turned this faucet to the side, water would drip next to the sink and run over the countertop to the floor.

We changed the system by positioning the T-section of the diversion so that the pedal-operated pump receives the water from the suction side of the pressure pump. The result is that the water only comes from the additional

faucet when we activate the pedal pump. We also added a three-way connector and an opening in the hull below the waterline, to take in saltwater. If you add it to the regular water for cooking rice, pasta or potatoes, or to pre-rinse the dirty dishes, you can save quite a bit of drinking water or stretch the supply.

EDGAR WOHLHEBEN, BY EMAIL

TIL THE LAST DROP

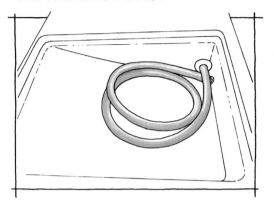

The normal position of the shower drain often makes it impossible to pump off all of the water. At least in our case, there is always a remaining unsightly pool of shower water. This can be avoided by adding a short, small hose with an opening angled to the drain opening. Now you can pump off the remaining water like a vacuum cleaner.

CHRISTOPH WALTHER, BY EMAIL

TIMELY ALERT

Fires on board at night are usually caused by inadvertent cable problems and are quite dangerous, due to the smoke. We mounted several battery-operated smoke alarms (about 20 dollars) to be safe.

HELMUT WENGLER, 14129 BERLIN

VENTILATED TOILET CASING

Usually the toilet sits in the center of the bathroom, and we didn't really like this design too much. So, we improved the look of this area with an appealing casing made from solid ledges and plywood, which also created additional small storage spaces for cleaning items and such. They can be accessed via small hatches in the top plate. To combat the unavoidable formation of mildew, due to humidity, we drilled four ventilation holes into the front face of the casing, but we realized that the air exchange was not enough. So, we added a small 12-Volt fan

(available at electronics retailers for a few dollars) to the front casing and framed the opening with a large metal ring. Such fans can be found in several sizes and they only consume about 100 milliamperes. The fan can be activated manually, using a timer or an interval switch.

As we use our engine on a regular basis I chose another method: the power is connected via a secure connection to the ignition lock. You should never use the connection to regulate the generator! As soon as we start the engine, the ventilation gets going.

HEINZ HAMANN, 21709 DUEDENBUETTEL

LESS HUMIDITY

We had some inconveniences with condensation humidity forming in the bow cabin and soaking everything. We added a very simple cover plate with magnetic latches. You should leave these plates open whenever you leave the boat for an extended period, to ventilate the cabin and to avoid mildew formation.

HEINZ HAMANN, 21709
DUEDENBUETTEL

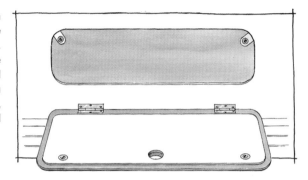

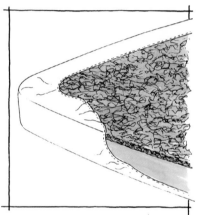

CLIMATE CONTROL FOR THE BUNK

When we were looking for an affordable base pad for our boat upholstery, we found a solution at a building supplies retailer. They are polypropylene mats, perfectly suited to ventilate the upholstery from below, and their price is quite reasonable. These mats can be placed onto the base of the bunk, or they can be cut to the size of the pads and fixed with the elastic band of fitted sheets.

STEFFEN STANKE, 26121 OLDENBURG

EFFECTIVE COOLING

In order to improve the air circulation in our cooler, we have added a small fan. We made a base plate from aluminum and placed it about a quarter-inch away from the evaporator. The fan blows air past an opening in the center of the plate onto the evaporator. Such fans are also used in computers. In order for it to run only when the cooler is running, it has to be connected parallel to the compressor and the thermostat.

JUDITH WUNDT, BY EMAIL

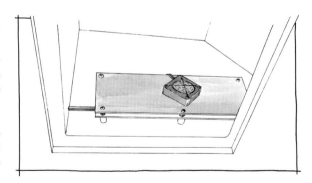

WORKSHOP &
WINTER STORAGE

LIGHT AROUND THE CORNER

Under difficult circumstances, it can be useful to shine a flashlight around a corner. If you wrap a transparent piece of hose with aluminum foil and tape, you can actually bend a light beam.
ROBERT BORCH, VIA EMAIL

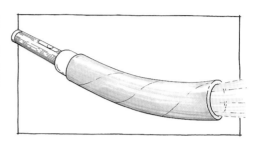

SIMPLE DIRT CATCHER

If you need to drill holes on board and don't have a vacuum cleaner handy, it is usually pretty annoying to try to remove the dirt caused by the drilling. You can use a simple coffee filter and tape it under the hole you need to drill, eliminating the need to clean up afterwards.
SASCHA LABUDA, 20095 HAMBURG

CLEAN BOOT TOP

Our boot top consists of a single-component paint applied on the GRP surface, and around autumn it is usually dirty, due to tar- and oil-containing substances. It was always rather difficult to clean it with thinner or spiritus. Last fall we were not able to complete this procedure, due to time constraints. We put the boat into the winter camp as it was.

This oversight was quite a problem when spring came along, because none of our efforts to clean it with products had any success. I observed that raindrops that had run down the hull left clean traces through the soiled boot top strip. We tried cleaning the boot top with a cloth and distilled water. To our surprise we were able to remove all of the deposits. It was shining as if brand new. In the spring we did not have to paint the boot top as we had planned.
INGO GRELLERT, 24235 LABOE

CLEANING THE TEAK DECK WITH AN ELECTRIC BRUSH

When cleaning teak decks, it is easy to make a mistake. Too much is as bad as too little. A practical high-pressure washer is great for removing even deep dirt, but it also damages the wood fiber itself. We also don't recommend treating it daily with a tough scrubber, particularly when working across the wood grain. The best solution is to perform an occasional "massage" with a soft brush against the grain—and that's not easy work! So, we found the following solution to make it easier: we screwed one of the base plates of our battery-powered sander to the back of a brush, so now we can connect the two with one simple click. The brown soup resulting from using the brush shows

how effective it is. You should never use a 110- or 220- Volt tool—they can be lethal!

HEINZ LORENZ, 84539 AMPFING

POLISHING MACHINE ON A RUBBER LINE

During summer, we usually wouldn't mind if the boat were a few feet longer, but as a skipper, when you get into winter repairs, you might curse every yard of the outer skin. Polishing the topsides with a machine is particularly work-intensive. Even though the machine can bring old gelcoats back to brilliance, the mere weight of the gear weakens your arms in no time. In order to make this work less daunting we tried hanging the machine from the railing with an elastic line. After some trial and error with different line diameters and lengths, we found a good combination. Now we only have to move the polishing machine up and down from its center position. We use two different lengths of elastic and we can polish the entire freeboard in about two days.

BERTHOLD SCHULZ, 22607 HAMBURG

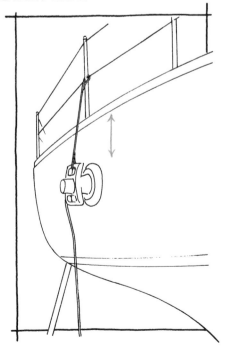

CHANGING IMPELLER WITH A STRAP

To replace the cooling pump impellers, we use a broad cable tie that we place over the center of the rubber wheel, so that its wings are bent and in working position. Tighten the cable tie, rotate it, and add some dishwashing soap to the wings. Now you can mount the impeller easily, even with one hand, while you gradually pull out the cable tie.
ROBERT KRINNER, 1030 VIENNA/AUSTRIA

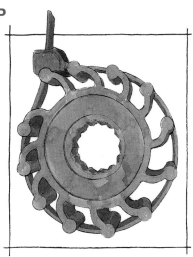

THE POWER OF CITRUS

The older your gelcoat, the more prone it is to getting yellowish lime deposits caused by algae. To remove it from the hull, we do not use expensive special cleaners but slices of lemon. They stick to the affected sections, and after 20 minutes the hull is white again. Depending on the deposit, six lemons are sufficient for a 32-foot yacht.
WILKO SCHOORMANNS, 24837 SCHLESWIG

FLEXIBLE SANDING BLOCK

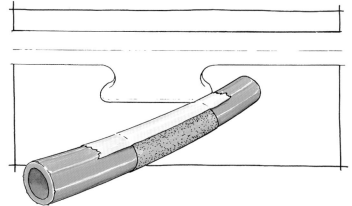

Varnished wood has to be taken care of sooner or later. You need to remove the old layer, or at least give it a good sanding. This is particularly annoying in the case of round sections of the handrail. We made a flexible sanding block for these intricate spots from a piece of sturdy garden hose. Put the sanding paper around the hose and tape it. The flexible hose adjusts its shape to any round surface with just a little pressure. You can also use fabric tubing, which is available in many different diameters.
MICHAEL KASTL, 22393 HAMBURG

SIMPLE LUBE

Modern shaft seals, like those made by Volvo Penta®, should be lubricated once a year. Although they offer a lube tube, it is too thick to be inserted between the rubber sleeve and the shaft. We use a disposable syringe with a thin, 1/8-inch diameter hose, which can be found at aquarium suppliers.

HELMUT WENGLER, BY EMAIL

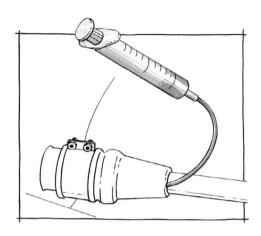

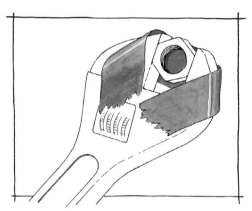

NUT ATTACHMENT

When you work on fittings, you often have to work in areas difficult to access. Positioning and holding nuts can quickly become a very arduous task. Because the stainless-steel nuts and bolts used on yachts are not magnetic, we have come up with the following trick: we affix the nut with a strip of tape to the tool. This makes it easy to place the nut without it disappearing into the bilge. A vise grip can also be used here.

DR. MORITZ KANZOW, 24103 KIEL

SPONGE BAG FOR LINES

You probably know the problem firsthand: lines full of algae that simply can't be put into a washing machine, because they are difficult to take off of the boat. For years we have been using the following trick. At the beginning of the season, we place the lines into a sturdy plastic bag and fill it with warm soapy water. We close the bag with a cable tie or a piece of line. After a day the halyards look like new. Just rinse thoroughly, and you are done.

LEONIE RICHTER, 50933 COLOGNE

AN EASIER WAY TO CLEAN YOUR TANK

When you put your yacht into its unheated winter quarters, you must clean and flush out the system's water supply lines with antifreeze. If you fail to do this, you risk damaging the pump, filter, faucets, or any of the lines with standing water, which may freeze and crack the surrounding material.

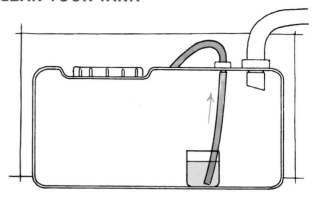

But you don't need to fill the entire freshwater tank with antifreeze just to rinse and clean the system. If the service opening is large enough, you can place a large glass of antifreeze into the tank, from which the pump sucks the liquid. When you do this, you may need to fill up the glass a few times, but the water will not taste of alcohol the following season. And since you only use a little antifreeze, you also save money.

SASCHA LABUDA, 20251 HAMBURG

NO MORE CLATTER

If you run your diesel engine towards the end of the season, you might be annoyed by the noise of the loose anode sitting on the shaft. I reduced the racket caused by this zinc block by adding cable ties on both sides of the shaft. They don't influence the operation of the shaft, because the cable ties are very lightweight. They eliminate any kind of clatter for good.

JOERN VOIGT, 22946 TRITTAU

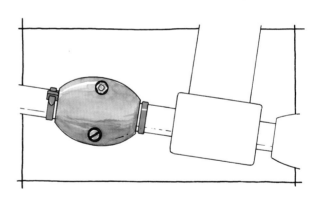

LONGER SHELF LIFE

Sealing compounds are essential on board, but you rarely need an entire tube. Once you open these tubes, they tend to harden with time, and after a few months, the entire tube could be as hard as stone. If you seal it airtight, the shelf life can be increased significantly. So, we unscrew the tip after each use, place a piece of cling wrap film over the opening, and then replace the tip.

JUDITH WUNDT, 24118 KIEL

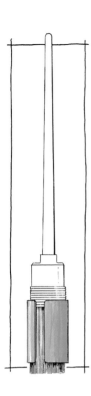

PAINT ISSUES

When paint brushes loose hairs, it is impossible to do a good varnishing job. So, you should rinse them before using them for the first time. They keep their shape if you place them into a bushing made from cut-up cable tubing. After using the brush and rinsing it with thinner, these sleeves prevent the brush from mushrooming. These sleeves can be used repeatedly.

PETER WILKEN, 26386 WILHELMSHAVEN

CAREFUL WITH THE PRESSURIZED WATER

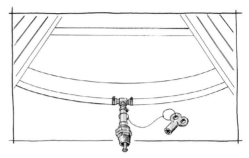

The remaining water in the pressurized water lines can cause quite some damage when the water freezes. At the lowest end of the water system we have installed a valve, like those used for heating installations, with its key right next to it. When the end of the season comes, we simply drain the water into the bilge and pick it up with a rag.

EDGAR WALLENBORN, 50171 KERPEN

FLUSHING THE ENGINE

Rinsing the engine and its seawater circuit, or adding antifreeze, whether on land or at sea, is quite an elaborate exercise and requires at least two people. Our flushing and rinsing method simplifies this process a lot and prevents spillage and even inundations. It consists of a large bucket with a conventional toilet water–intake limiter mounted inside. The outer side features a standard garden hose snap connector (like a Gardena®) for fresh water supply. The engine side is connected via a faucet, such as those you may find on rainwater barrels. Now you can connect the engine, even with a full bucket, without spilling. You simply mix the antifreeze into the water of the bucket.

JOACHIM SCHIEMANN, BY EMAIL

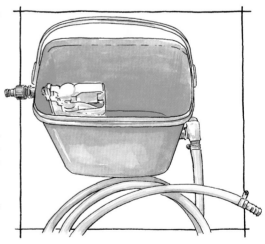

ENGINE FLUSH

When we prepare our boat for winter storage, we first flush the cooling circuit with fresh water and then fill it with antifreeze and anticorrosion liquid. To keep the bilge clean while doing this, we made an additional hose connection for the seawater filter. Remove the sight glass of the filter and replace it with an equally sized piece of Plexiglas®, with an inserted brass hose connector fitted in and sealed with Sikaflex®. Using the

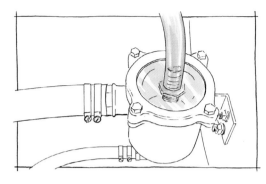

additional hose, while the engine is running, we first add fresh water and then antifreeze to the cooling system. Once the engine is flushed completely, we put back the original sight glass of the filter.

HELMUT NEUMANN, 32108 BAD SALZUFLEN

WATER CONNECTION

For easy servicing of our cooling system, we added a two-way valve. The pictured system does not require you to close the seawater valve. Just connect the flushing hose and open the two-way valve. This allows the antifreeze to flush the system until it exits the exhaust pipe. Another positive effect: the impeller does not run dry, as there is always water being sucked into the circuit.

JUERGEN KRUSE, BY EMAIL

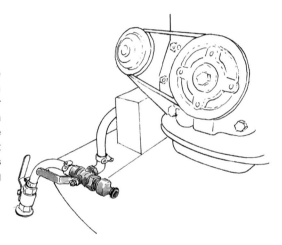

HOSE REPAIR

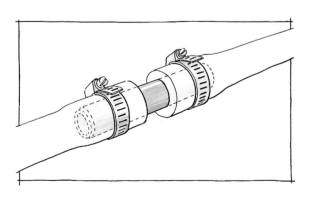

If you have a leak in your engine cooling system, it is game over. You should always have a short section of tube and two hose clamps handy for repair. If the leak is in a straight section, cut out the damaged section and place the tube in its place, securing it with the clamps. If the leak is at a bent section, or where you have a fixed and rusty pipe elbow, it may be more difficult. Dry the section, remove any clamps, put on an even layer of sealant, and wrap a gauze around it. Repeat this procedure until you have a watertight layer.

M. G. KUEPPER, 77652 OLDENBURG

FIXING A LEAKY BILGE

The integrated vent valve on the coolant intake becomes a nuisance when it continually leaks small amounts of water, as it steadily creates humidity in the bilge. Here is what you can do: either add a connecting hose to a collection container placed in the engine compartment, or install an automatic fan with an integrated float.
GERD EHRICH, 40789 MOHNHEIM

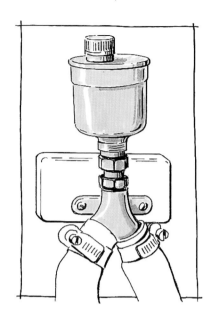

GALLOWS FOR THE YACHT

Let's say your boat is standing in your shed or open-air winter space. When you used the pressure washer on your antifouling paint, several pieces were blown away. You have no choice: the old layers have added up and become too thick and brittle, so you have to peel off the layer down to the gelcoat and put on a new one.

Once you are done with the required preparation, you should add osmosis protection as well. As this requires several layers of epoxy, the hull supports and their contact areas become a problem. How do you paint these spots?

We found a simple solution. As the main weight of the yacht rests on its keel, it can be secured without these supports. We added several poles tied to the toe rails and "hung" the boat from them. For additional stability, these poles can be connected with diagonal braces, using screws.

You should never remove all four of the original hull supports—no more than two per side, or the front or the rear ones. This assures a secure position of the boat.
DIETMAR WURR, 24768 RENDSBURG

HELP WITH GLUE

Gluing and sealing compounds are very strong and durable, but they take quite some time to cure, so the pieces need to be fixated well. If you cannot use clamps, tape, or other items, here is a trick: leave some small areas untreated and then fill them with hot glue. It cools down immediately after pressing the section together and holds them firmly in place, until the rest of the glue has cured and hardened.

WOLFGANG HASS, 6300 ZUG/SCHWEIZ

NON-STICK SEAL

You may have experienced this already: you want to divvy out the content of a paint container and keep a small amount on board for reparation work, so you pour the paint or varnish into a jam jar. About a week later you can hardly open it. We put some lube spray on the rim of the glass. This allows you to open the jar even much later.

HANS-PETER MUEHLHOFF, 42349 WUPPERTAL

GOUGING TOOL

The deck of our 20-year-old Aphrodite 33 was badly weathered, and its sealant stuck out about 1/16 of an inch over the wood. Whenever we walked on the deck, we felt this spongy feeling, and there was the possibility it ripping off, too. To remove excess material, we found that a cheese slicer worked best. Better to get several of them, however, because they only work while they're sharp. Slide the cutter of the slicer in line with the wood grain and apply a little pressure flat over the wood. If you catch the teak wood with the cutter, stop immediately and trace back; you can glue the splint later with epoxy. Before

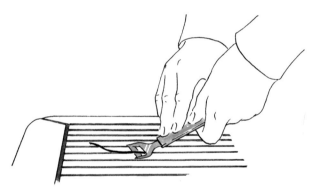

finishing the job, run a sander over the surface to even out minor differences between the sealant and the deck.

PETER WURST, 63667 NIDDA

PUMP CONTROL

Many boats feature an automatic bilge pump, so minor leaks remain unnoticed as the pump removes the leaked water.

Because even the smallest leaks can be an indication of an upcoming problem, we added a warning light for the bilge pump at the cockpit. It is connected parallel to the pump at the floater and indicates an active pump.

ACHIM MUELLER, 52538 GANGELTW

FOLD IT AWAY

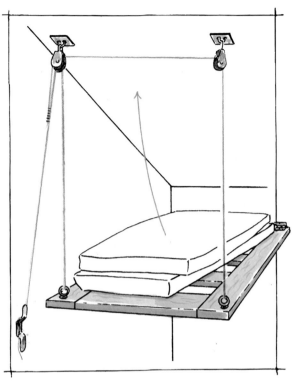

There are quite a few items you take from the boat in autumn, just to put them back in spring: pads, various sails, rubber dinghy, etc. We almost ran out of space in our basement. Fortunately the ceiling is pretty high, creating a perfect place to store these items. We built a flat frame from plywood boards and bolted the short end, with hinges, to the wall. The frame is smooth, so items can slide on and off. The hinges allow for the frame to be lowered to make it easier to load items, and two pulleys guide two lines to the wall. Knot both lines together and tie them to a cleat on the wall. This makes it really easy to lower and raise the platform. If you want to store rather heavy items, you might want to support the lower part of the frame with aluminum angles, which also help to prevent twisting, and use a trailer winch or a pulley with a Camcleat®.

ACHIM MUELLER, 52538 GANGELT

THIS & THAT

HALYARD TO CLEAN THE LOG

If your speedometer shows a value of zero, it might be because it does not get an impulse from the log. Even thin threads of algae can result in faults and wrong data. Try this simple trick to clean the log. Bring a line under the bow and gently pull it back and forth. If you manage to move the log, it usually continues to work. It is best to stop the propeller while doing this.

HASSO KIRSTEIN, 22119 HAMBURG

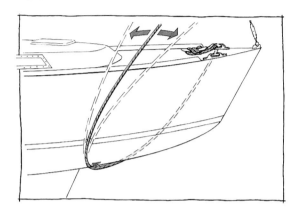

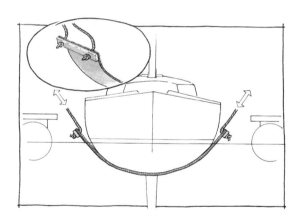

UNDERWATER SCRUBBER

If you do not use an antifouling coat, you will have to clean your hull on a regular basis. This is quite a job, but you can make it easier by taking a broad strip of artificial lawn (AstroTurf®), affix it to two sturdy ledges with loops, and pull them back and forth under the boat's hull, like a giant scrubber. This is quite effective for removing growth and dirt.

HELMUT ELFEBER, 58239 SCHWERTE

SUPPORT LINES FOR DIVES

If you have to dive under the boat, perhaps to clear a line from the propeller, you will use most of your energy and air trying to stay under water. One or several lines around the hull will save you from wriggling around. It is much easier to get to where you need to be and to stay there. You can also secure tools using the lines.

FRITZ KELLER, 22850 NORDERSTEDT

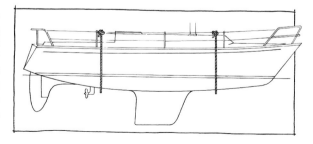

GRIP HELP

If your bottom sprayhood or cockpit is affixed via tough elastic slings, they have to be fairly tight. If you use your fingers to remove them from their hooks, you need to apply quite some force, and you might break a fingernail. Just leave a short, permanent loop of string knotted into the elastic line to avoid hurting your fingertips.

FROM *YACHT* 20/99

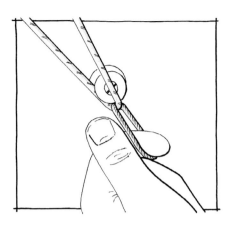

PROTECTOR FOR LOG IMPELLER

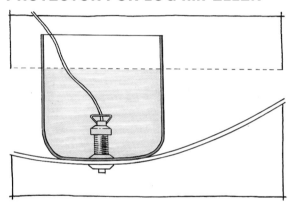

If the log does not work, you should first check for foreign objects. But even experienced skippers cannot avoid splashing a good measure of water out from the tube, which then flows into the bilge. If you add a plastic container around the impeller tube, such as a cut-up canister, you can pick up the excess water.

KARL-HEINZ GRUENEBERG, 24235 LABOE

A BRIGHTER FLAME

We only have one battery on board. Because we use kerosene to cook, it was only logical to also use a kerosene lamp as a position and anchor light. This is fine while inside the cabin, but we sometimes wondered whether it was safe enough to use outside. While anchoring during the night, we would have liked to make sure that other ships noticed us.

This problem was solved when we learned that adding 5% worth of spiritus to the kerosene would improve its burn. The first test was rather convincing: not only was the flame a lot brighter, but there was also a lot less soot coming from the flame. There is some kind of residue at the bottom of the tank, however, so remove it whenever necessary.

EDGAR HARTMAN, 10963 BERLIN

LAMP LIGHT BLOWER

Many petroleum lamps cannot be blown out easily. Whether you hold your hand behind the flame or not, the air is just not sufficient to extinguish it. If you use a plastic tube with a thin end, you can direct the air precisely towards the flame of the lamp.

HELMUT WENGLER, 14129 BERLIN

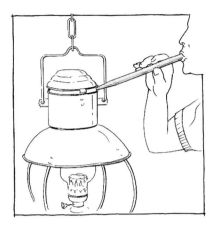

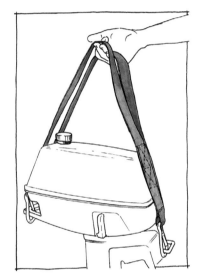

SAFETY LINE AS CARRYING HELP

Whenever the outboarder produces more than the standard two or three horsepower, it becomes rather laborious to lower the engine down the stern to the dinghy. The engines also tend to be more difficult to handle. There are special carrying straps available, but you can also use the lifeline with two carabiner hooks latched to the front and back of the motor.

ACHIM WECKLER, 65795 HATTERSHEIM

WELL LATCHED

Instead of using lines to tie down everything while towing the trailer, you can also use oversized cable ties. They don't slacken, they don't have to be re-tightened, and can be used repeatedly.

KONNY BARTELS, 28197 BREMEN

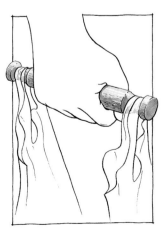

CARRYING HELP

When you walk away from the supermarket, those plastic bags cut pretty deep into the sailor's already worn hands. A simple solution is to make a carrying strap from a piece of round wood and carve notches at the ends, so the bags don't slip off. This won't lighten the burden, but it will help to carry it!

SEEN IN FLENSBURG

PROTECTION FROM SEAGULLS

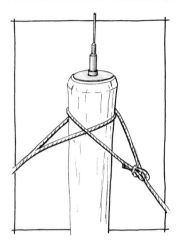

Seagulls love to hold their siesta on the stern poles of our moorings. However, they have this ritual of relieving themselves just before going out for another catch. The result is, when you return after a week, the stern lines are covered with acidic seagull droppings. The simplest solution would be to drive a few nails into the top of the pole, but the port managers frown upon that. So, we made a defense gadget from an old soap suction hose and a useless CD, by gluing them together and placing the thing onto the pole. It works like a charm.

KARL-HEINZ GRUENEBERG, 24235 LABOE

SOFT PROJECTILE

Throwing a line to another boat is no big deal when the weather is fair and the water is calm; a strong thrower and a nicely coiled line is all it takes. But with a stiff breeze and choppy waters, the story is quite different. This is where you need some sort of weight added to the line. You need to get to the other boat, perhaps to tow one of the boats. Do not use hard items such as blocks or winches, as they will damage the boat—and the person who has to catch the line. You can quickly and easily make a throwing weight by filling a sock with rice. You can throw it quite far and it will not hurt anyone.

HEINZ BAUER, 38162 CREMLINGEN

QUICK CHECK

If you charter a yacht, some people say it is more than just a good idea to inspect the hull's underwater section. The yacht charter agencies often use a diver for the job, but for the customer, it's more complicated. The watertight case of my Sony® digital camera inspired me to figure out how to avoid a dive in dirty port waters. I just placed the camera onto the closed tripod and tied the tripod to a boathook.

Now you can inspect the entire hull in little time and check the result on the spot. You can make detailed shots and do a before-and-after comparison.

AXEL AUGSPURGER, 15711 KOENIGS WUSTERHAUSEN

MEMORY AIDS

Just how did I run the pulleys from the mast to the cockpit? If you don't take detailed notes, you often have to go through the trial-and-error method again when the next season starts. This applies to many areas on board, including the electronics inside of the mast.

We take photos before taking down the mast to use as memory aids and reminders. When the next season comes, we print out the photos on our color printer, which we always bring along in its waterproof bag, so it is no problem to compare the details.

If the laptop computer is part of the onboard equipment, you can keep a log and save the photos to it.

HOLGER NAUJOK, 24939 FLENSBURG

SUCTION TUBE FACILITATES TRANSFER

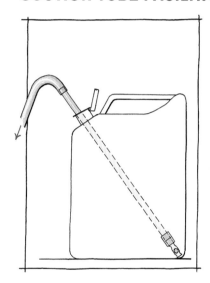

You see him at all the trade fairs: "Mr. Quick-Fix" showing off his hose, fitted with a ball valve, that facilitates the fuel transfer from the jerrican into the tank. A few up and down movements of the valve inside the jerrican takes up fuel into the hose, until the level surpasses the zenith of the bent hose. From then on the fuel flows by itself until the jerrican is empty. There are many copycats following the same method, whose products work. Unfortunately they all run into the same problem whenever the hose inside the jerrican bends upwards, due to it being rolled up during storage, and its opening ends up above the surface of the fuel. Once it sucks in air, the transfer of fuel is over. So, we have added a fixed tube and now we can transfer the fuel to the last drop.

HERBERT SEITZ, 83119 OBING

FILLING UP WITHOUT SPILLS

To fill the integrated tank of our small outboarder while on tour, I use a bottle with the exact same volume as the tank to avoid spillage. I place the neck of the bottle into the tank opening—no spill. Just make sure that the fuel tank is completely empty, or there will be spills. A transparent bottle is helpful. I use a hose or a funnel to fill the bottle.

RUDOLF SCHNEITER, 78343 GAIENHOFEN/ BODENSEE

FILLING WITHOUT SPILLING

Most dinghy engines have an integrated tank. Even with the utmost care, you cannot always avoid spilling a few drops. This usually means you have to use a liquid soap bottle to remove the drop of fuel from the water. We avoid such inconveniences by using a homemade filling system. The main piece is a rubber pump with valves, usually used between the external tank of an outboarder and the engine. The pump is used to move the fuel out of the jerrican. We fitted a closing valve to the end of the hose, which helps to refuel without spilling a single drop. Once the tank is full, you simply close the end valve and lift up the hose while pumping the remaining fuel in the hose

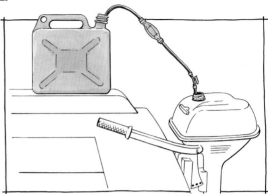

back into the jerrican. We keep a rag handy to pick up fuel drops.

HAND MUEHLBAUER, 86165 AUGSBURG

A BUCKET OF WATER TO ASSIST REFUELING

It takes quite a bit of practice and experience to avoid spillage when refueling diesel. The large nozzles are quite difficult to handle, and refueling from a canister or jerrican almost guarantees a spill. There is a well-known trick for preserving the teak deck from permanent soiling, which involves pouring a bucket of water on the deck before refueling. We also use this trick on decks made from GRP. The logic here is that the water causes the spilled diesel fuel to swim on top of the water, so it doesn't stick to the surface of the deck, where it can only be removed using chemicals. This method makes it easy to simply pick out the water containing diesel using paper towels or other water-absorbing material.

HANS MUEHLBAUER, 86165 AUGSBURG

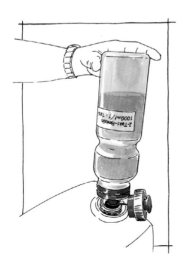

CLEAN FILLING

To refuel our small outboarder, we use a bicycle bottle. The bottle should be transparent, if possible, made from PE, and feature a large opening lid for refilling, as well as a small opening that can be closed. Of course, you would need to label this bottle, as it is originally intended for beverages.

GÜNTER NOLDE, 56070 KOBLENZ

MOBILE SUCTION CUP FOR LISTING BOAT

Many yachts have their share of a minimum amount of water inside the boat. Even modern GRP boats have a good bucket of water sloshing around the bilge, although nowadays this is not necessary. There are many shaft seal systems available today that are totally waterproof, but there are still interior sources on board, such as pressure valves on the hot water boiler, ventilation in the cooling water lines, or small leaks in the fresh water pressure system. These sources of water are easy to fix. But then there are those leaks caused by fittings on deck that you have to track down and fix. It is actually possible to have a bone-dry bilge.

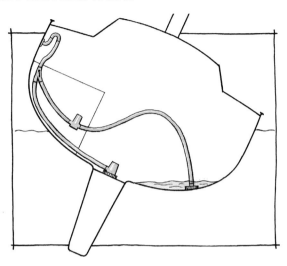

Nevertheless, all seagoing vessels are fitted with a bilge pump system with a suction intake inside the bilge, but in daily practice this system will be of little use. There are many boat designs that no longer have a real bilge, where leaking water was able to collect around a suction intake. Even a slight list will cause the water to slosh around the hull; it might even reach behind the cabinets or shoot up the cabin wall, where delicate electronics might be mounted. For situations like this, we have added a second pumping system with an electric pump and a mobile suction head we can position anywhere on the boat, independent of the current list.

HANS PROCKERT, BY EMAIL

AUXILIARY ENGINE AT THE STERN

Did you catch a net or a line with your propeller? Situations like this one are pretty problematic for sailors, even though the engine is only an auxiliary item. After several annoying experiences, we built a support out of plywood, so we could use our outboarder from the bathing platform. We found out that we can maneuver our Bavaria 350 with our dinghy outboarder. The 2.5-hp engine of our Mercury provides some 1.5 knots of speed, which is fine for careful port maneuvers, provided the wind does not blow too hard from the wrong direction. The system consists of a permanent base plate with integrated bolts sticking out, to which the support of the motor itself is affixed with wing nuts. The base plate is not in the way when using the bathing

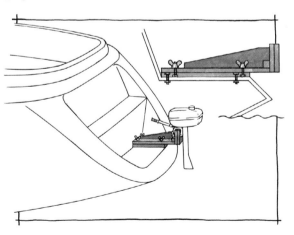

platform, and when the bolts are not in use they are covered with dome nuts.

GERD EHRICH, 40789 MONHEIM

ENGINE TRANSPORT

An outboarder engine is great to have if you want to maneuver around the port with your boat. Unfortunately, it is almost impossible to transport the outboarder with a car without getting it dirty and smelly. We avoid this problem by putting the auxiliary engine outside. Simply place it onto the crossbeam in front of the keel support. To avoid scratching the engine paint, you can use belts to hang it from the support; this will avoid any contact with parts of the trailer. You should add a piece of wood to make sure that the bolts of the engine are tightened extremely well, and you should always check both the belts and the tightening bolts after driving for a few miles. Another advantage is that there is more space for luggage in your vehicle. If you

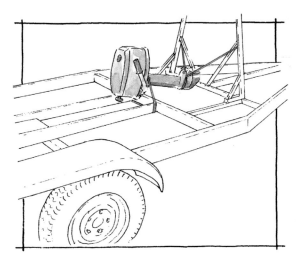

plan to leave the trailer unattended, make sure you secure it against theft.

HANS-JOERG WIEDEMANN, 10715 BERLIN

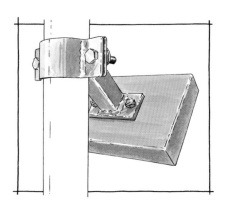

OUTBOARDER UNDER DECK

Trailing a boat usually means that your car is crammed. On our Sun 2000 we transport our outboarder on a special support, affixed to the mast support, inside the cabin. This also protects the engine from bad weather and thieves.

WOLFGANG BOERNER, 85609 ASCHHEIM

LADDER AS GRILL SUPPORT

People usually don't use a charcoal grill on their boats, due to the danger of falling embers that damage the deck or the ship's side. Often the outriggers are too short, anyway. If you have a bathing platform and a ladder, you can use it as an extension of the outrigger. Just tighten the line so the grill is over the water and still easy to reach.

PETER BADS, BY EMAIL

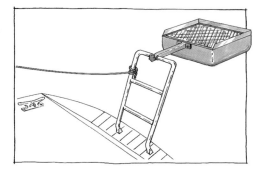

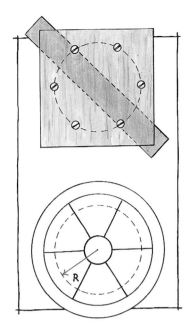

TANK CAP OPENER

In your special section about "Drinking Water" (YACHT 8/04), you mentioned large inspection hatches for the tanks. However, their screwed-on lids need to be handled delicately for them to close tightly. Even with small differences in temperature, they tend to get stuck, and you need to apply quite some force to open them. For these situations, we built ourselves a robust opener with a grip. There are some six screws sticking out about half an inch from the bottom of the grip; they allow the lid to be turned without damaging it.

PETER ZIMPEL, 14089 BERLIN

THE NEXT TRIP

The last journey was months ago, the preparations for the next one are entering the hot phase. You meet with the crew and exchange ideas and information. Experience shows that all this information and hearsay tends to be forgotten rather quickly. For many years we have kept our own form on the computer. Every piece of information is reflected in this form: the new restaurant at a mooring place, cheap outlets for buying supplies, and so forth. We keep this list updated during and after the journey. When the trip is over, we add additional data, print it out, and give a copy to everyone.

HORST SCHAEFFER, 70195 STUTTGART

CLIMATE PROTECTION FOR THE BOAT

If you have to keep your boat outside for an extended period of time and can't service or clean it on a regular basis, your best choice is to cover the boat with a tarp. This applies to the winter quarter on land as well as mooring at port. The worst enemy here is the wind; it is easy for it to cause destruction, due to large surfaces. If your tarps are too thin, you will soon find them in tatters. Even the strongest truck-type tarp will survive permanent friction for only a short time—for example, when the tarp is fastened over the railing supports. So, we tension the tarp down to the edge of the deck, as it reduces the area where the wind can do a lot of damage. Our boat does not feature a toe rail, so to replace it, we simply tie a strong ledge to the bottom of the railing from the outside. Securing the tarp with a long line along its entire length helps a lot.

INGEBORG CLASEN, 22605 HAMBURG

HOSE FOR THE EXHAUST PIPE

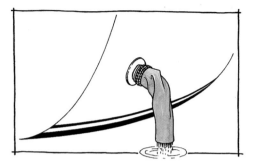

If you don't like the noisy bubbling from the exhaust pipe of your yacht, not to mention the soot, you have to use a hose. Hoses are prone to catching lines and fenders, however, and you might break it off at one of the poles while maneuvering out of the box. I made a flexible hose from a piece of canvas, affixed with a rubber band, and a line. This way your muffler is well protected.

HEINZ HAMANN, 21709 DUEDENBUETTEL

DROP CATCHER

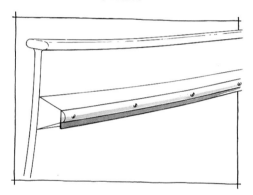

You can notice air and water pollution by looking at the black rainwater streaks that form at the hull after just a few days. Even if you have scuffing ribs with integrated drip-off, you cannot really prevent this from happening. We came up with the idea to slightly loosen the brass ribs we had added to protect the wood and slid a narrow plastic ledge from the bottom until it touched the screws. Once you re-tighten the screws, it is kept in place by the brass rib and works great as a drip-off. We have no more annoying and hard-to-remove dirt on our hull.

HORST TESCHKE, 27572 BREMERHAVEN

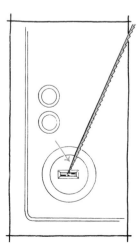

BROKEN KEY - NOW WHAT?

A broken key isn't such a huge problem if you keep a spare one. But the real problem is, how do you get the remaining piece out of the lock's cylinder? We tried using a fretsaw blade that we sharpened so it can easily be inserted into the cylinder. The saw's teeth act like barbs, so the rest of the key can be pulled out.

KLAUS PETER, 89520 HEIDENHEIM

CLEAN HULL THANKS TO DROPSTOP®

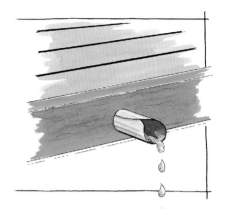

We are always annoyed by the black water streaks on the hull after every rainstorm. In particular the area below the scuppers was rather unsightly. To prevent the rain from running along the hull when you are moored for some time, use DropStop® discs. These small plastic discs are supposed to prevent wine from spilling when pouring out of a bottle, by providing a clean top-off edge. Rather than putting them into bottles, we put these handy discs into each scupper of our wooden deck ledges. The resulting tubes feed the water away from the hull so there is no more staining to complain about.

ESTHER STETTLER, 3645 GWATT/SWITZERLAND

DOLLY FOR THE DINGHY

We have a buoy mooring space at Lake Constance, so the only way to get to the yacht is by dinghy. That would not be a problem if it were not for the annoying transport of the dinghy on land. So, I started looking for a solution with wheels. The stock solutions were either too expensive or did not fit my concept, but eventually I found a folding dolly. I sawed off the handles and mounted it to the dinghy's transom, so once I am inside the dinghy, I can flip up the wheels. The only disadvantage is that I cannot mount an outboarder anymore, but I don't need

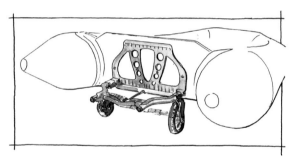

one for the short trip to the yacht—I can just use an oar.

GERHARD RITTER, 71404 KORB

NIGHT PASSAGE WITHOUT GLARE

When you are at port or moored, it is always nice to have bright interior lighting. However, when you are sailing at night, your eyes take about 20 to 30 minutes to adjust to the darkness. And bright light eliminates this adjustment in the blink of an eye. A good alternative is red light—this color interferes the least with retinal adjustment. If you only do occasional nighttime outings, you don't need to change your lamps. We simply place a piece of red foil behind the glass cover of the lamp.

CHRISTIAN FEIGE, 94469 DEGGENDORF

WOODEN BIRD KEEPS THE SPRAYHOOD CLEAN

Seagulls love cockpits and sprayhoods as resting places. But they leave ugly acid "presents" on the GRP and the tarpaulin cover. To avoid serious staining, we use a model of a flying blackbird to scare away the seagulls. The replica, made from thin and lightweight wood, is painted black and has a wingspan of about three feet. Before leaving the boat we hang it at the boom head. This method keeps the cockpit and the tarpaulin clean, even during longer mooring.

DIETER NEUBECKER, 24568 KALTENKIRCHEN

TRICK FOR THE DINGHY

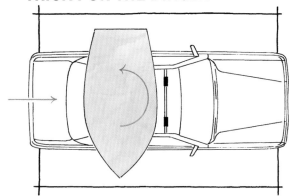

When two people are lifting the dinghy onto the roofrack, it is much easier to do it at a 90-degree angle, carry it from the rear to its position, and only then turn it around to face the front. You can lift it up easily, because the bow and the stern of the dinghy stick out over the width of the vehicle. When you take it off the roof, just reverse the process.

HORST REINDL, 85757 KARLSFELD

CHAFING PROTECTOR FOR THE TARPAULIN

We prevent the winter tarpaulin, with or without mounted railing, from chafing by using PVC tubes, such as those utilized for home heating installations. First drill these at the correct distance to the railing supports, then cut them lengthwise with a circular hand saw. You only need to tie them up. This system provides a nice round edge around the hull.

PETER AXEN, 23570 LUEBECK-TRAVEMUENDE

HOW TO KEEP CLOTHING FRESH ON BOARD

When you store folded T-shirts, underwear, and other articles of clothing on board, they tend to become musty and damp. Whenever we prepare for a long journey, we place the dry clothing into large freezer bags and seal them using a heat sealer. The clothes don't wrinkle and they are nice and fresh when you take them out of their protective bags. You can store unopened bags like this for the next trip.

HEIDRUN BABIK, 44892 BOCHUM

STRONG PINS

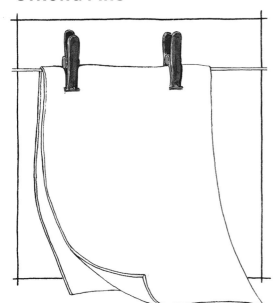

If you've ever tried to hang pieces of carpet or sailing jackets from the railing to dry, then you know that conventional clothespins do not provide the required grip. We found sturdy clamps at a hardware store, such as those used for carpentry work; they are perfect for overweight textiles. You can find a cheap six-pack of these clamps for just a few dollars. Due to their size, they can pin even thick fabrics safely to the line, and they also have very strong springs, so we also use them for drying wet towels. We've never had a piece of clothing get away from the grip of these clamps.

HELLMUT KOCH, 38100 BRAUNSCHWEIG

CABLE SUPPORT

Round cables are dangerous, both on deck and at the port. If you step on them, they roll away and you might fall. If you tie the shown clips to the cable with cable ties, you can hang them from the railing without any problem, and the deck is free of potential hazards. We tie the cable ties loosely, so we can use this system at any port and slide them into place.

FELIX NEUKORN, 8353 ELGG/
SWITZERLAND

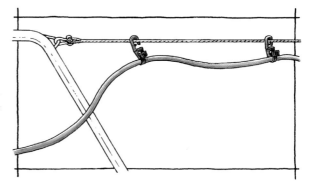

ANTI-REFLECTION TRICK

Bright surfaces and fittings can cause irritating reflections on the boat's instruments. You might not be able to read them correctly, if at all.

Due to the trend towards glossy displays, this is a common problem, not only with instruments on board, but cell phones, cameras, and tablets as well. Anti-reflection covers and protecting foils for tablets are available, and they work very well for other instrumentation displays as well. They are not expensive and you might be able to cover two instruments with one. They stick without any glue and can be removed without leaving any residue. They also protect against scratches.

SEBASTIAN IBBEKEN, 12203 BERLIN

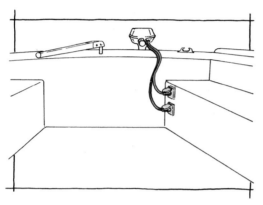

POWER SUPPLY

We use welding connectors to run the electric lines from the outboarder to the battery in the storage locker. They are capable of handling high loads and are also weather resistant. Don't forget to mark the polarity; if you connect the cables the wrong way, the motor will not run.

LUKAS GEERS, 49413 DINKLAGE

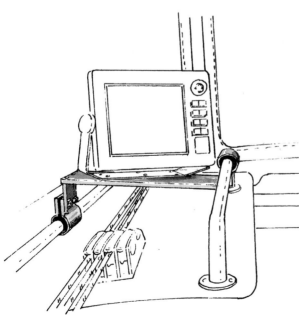

MOBILE PLOTTER

Our chart plotter is not exactly light, so we did not want to mount it on the steering column, but rather, under the sprayhood. We made an L-shaped bridge from thin aluminum sheet (1/16 inch). The edges are bent so the sheet is less flexible. We used four pipe clamps to affix the bridge to the handrails. A standard mounting bracket, fastened to the bridge with a knurled screw, holds the plotter. A slit allows for the plotter to be turned and moved along this slit so the screen can be positioned as needed. When at port, we simply remove the plotter and store it in the cabin.

EDGAR OHNMACHT, 27283 VERDEN

CENTERING HELP

It is not exactly a piece of cake to slip your boat onto the trailer without it running off-center at the last moment. We have built auxiliary frames from wood and affixed them to the trailer so they are positioned just before the widest section of the hull. Two lines are used to stabilize them. This prevents the boat from getting away from the center line of the trailer.

PHILINE PESCHKE, 22605 HAMBURG

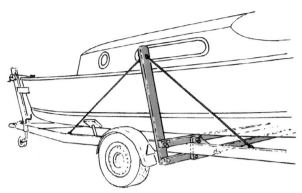

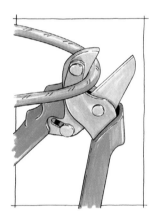

SINGLE-HANDED CUTS

Cutting lines and halyards is often quite difficult. We use a set of brand new garden shears. They are particularly useful when cutting under water, such as when our stern line gets caught in the propeller. You only need two or three cuts to solve this problem. Contrary to using a knife, these special pliers virtually eliminate the risk of injury. Make sure you lubricate the hinge regularly.

DIETER ROSKE, 34346 HANN. MUENDEN

COMFORTABLE REMOTE CONTROL

To control the outboarder without any twisting and turning from the cockpit, we built an extension for the gear shift. We screwed an angled section of steel below the grip. It serves as the center of rotation for the new lever, also made from steel sheet metal. Both are connected via a round rod with fork heads. You can also use a thin shroud turnbuckle.

TONI PETERS, BY EMAIL

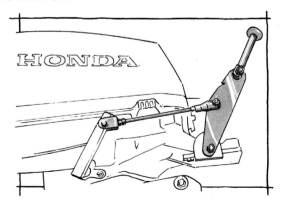

MOSQUITO NET FOR THE LADDERWAY

As soon as a summer day ends, mosquitos tend to show up. While it is easy to protect windows and hatches, the ladderway is a proper landing strip for these bloodsuckers. We came up with a construction consisting of a piece of net curtain, two wooden ledges cut to fit the hatch guide, and some lead line. Clip the wooden ledges onto the curtain and hook them behind the guiding rails on both sides. The lead line at the lower end keeps it in place.

DIANA MEHL, 41363 JUECHEN

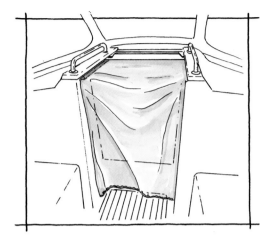

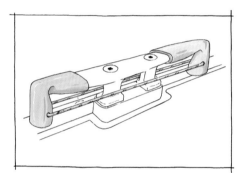

PROTECTED CLEAT

Cleats and clamps are great for mooring a boat, but while you're sailing, they can be rather annoying, as they tend to attract halyards at the wrong moment and become stuck. We solved this problem by adding two short sections of hose and sliding them over the hooks. Bend down the ends until they touch the deck, and add a rubber sling so they stay in place.

SEEN IN GELTING-MOLE

INDEX